P9-CRZ-255

Girls Who Rocked the World

HEROINES FROM JOAN OF ARC TO MOTHER TERESA

**MICHELLE ROEHM McCANN
& AMELIE WELDEN**

ALADDIN
New York London Toronto Sydney New Delhi

BEYOND WORDS
Hillsboro, Oregon

ALADDIN
An imprint of Simon & Schuster
Children's Publishing Division
1230 Avenue of the Americas
New York, NY 10020

BEYOND WORDS
20827 N.W. Cornell Road, Suite 500
Hillsboro, Oregon 97124-9808
503-531-8700 / 503-531-8773 fax
www.beyondword.com

This Aladdin/Beyond Words edition October 2012

Text copyright © 1998, 2009, 2012 by Amelie Welden
Text copyright © 2000 by Michelle Roehm
Text copyright © 2012 by Michelle R. McCann
Interior illustrations copyright © 2012 by Beyond Words Publishing, Inc.

Portions of this work were previously published in an earlier edition of *Girls Who Rocked the World* and in *Girls Who Rocked the World 2*.

All rights reserved, including the right of reproduction in whole or in part in any form.
ALADDIN is a trademark of Simon & Schuster, Inc., and related logo is a registered
trademark of Simon & Schuster, Inc.
Beyond Words Publishing is an imprint of Simon & Schuster, Inc. and related logo is a registered
trademark of Beyond Words Publishing, Inc.

For information about special discounts for bulk purchases, please contact
Simon & Schuster Special Sales at 1-866-506-1949 or business@simonandschuster.com.

The Simon & Schuster Speakers Bureau can bring authors to your live event.
For more information or to book an event contact the Simon & Schuster Speakers Bureau at
1-866-248-3049 or visit our website at www.simonspeakers.com.

Managing editor: Lindsay S. Brown
Editors: Emmalisa Sparrow, Ali McCart
Interior design: Sara E. Blum
Interior illustrations: David Hahn
The text of this book was set in Adobe Garamond Pro.
The illustrations for this book were rendered in Adobe Illustrator.

Manufactured in the United States of America 0716 MTN

10 9 8

Library of Congress Cataloging-in-Publication Data

McCann, Michelle Roehm,
    Girls who rocked the world : heroines from Anne Frank to Natalie Portman /
    Michelle Roehm McCann and Amelie Welden.
        p.   cm.
    Includes bibliographical references.
    1. Girls—Biography—Juvenile literature.   2. Women heros—Biography—Juvenile
    literature.   3. Heros—Biography—Juvenile literature. I. Welden, Amelie, 1975– II. Title.
CT3207.M34   2012
920.72—dc23
                                                                                        2011050502

ISBN 978-1-58270-302-2 (pbk)
ISBN 978-1-58270-361-9 (hc)
ISBN 978-1-4424-5182-7 (eBook)

For Fiona, my amazing girl.
I can't wait to see how you
will rock the world.
—Michelle

To all the many girls and women who've
inspired me throughout my life.
—Amelie

We stand at the beginning of a new epoch in the history of humankind's thought, as we recognize that...woman, like man, makes and defines history.

—GERDA LERNER, PROFESSOR OF HISTORY, UNIVERSITY OF WISCONSIN

CONTENTS

⁓⁓⁓

In the profiles in this book, passages of literary narrative based on factual events were imagined by the authors in an attempt to draw the reader into the life and perspective of the profiled girl.

Note from the Authors

The future belongs to those who believe in the beauty of their dreams.

—ELEANOR ROOSEVELT

What if we asked you to name some important people from history—who would you list? If you're like most of us, you'd probably name more men than women. (If not, good for you!) But why do most people think of men when they consider influential people in history? Is it because women weren't important? No way! Women's strength, ingenuity, and perseverance have always been vital in defining the world's cultures and civilizations. It's just that many stories of women and girls have been left out of traditional history that gets recorded and taught.

Luckily, in recent years, progress has been made toward restoring women's roles in history. Most of you have read plenty of stories about amazing grown women and their achievements—Amelia Earhart, Susan B. Anthony, Rosa Parks—and you probably thought to yourselves, *Hey, when I grow up, maybe I can do something important like that!* While our current history books are giving more credit to women from the past, it is equally important that you, today's girls, know that you can make your own impact on the history books of tomorrow.

With *Girls Who Rocked the World*, we want to show that you don't have to wait until you grow up. The girls in this book didn't wait until they were adults to start rocking the world.

And rocking the world doesn't necessarily mean you have to become famous and fabulously rich. It can mean you took a chance, made a change, inspired someone, stood up for yourself, ignored your critics, changed a person's mind, or comforted someone. It means you didn't just sit back and let the world rock you.

With these issues in mind, we set to work on *Girls Who Rocked the World*. We are proud to be a part of retelling the history of many amazing girls and hope that our work encourages you to believe in your dreams and in your power to make a difference.

With so many incredible girls out there, deciding who to include was pretty difficult. We chose girls who left their mark on history—or seriously began on their path—before the age of twenty and who reflect a diversity of countries, time periods, and achievements. Although the heroines in this book come from every corner of the globe and rocked the world in totally different ways, they do have a few important things in common. Each overcame obstacles—poverty, lack of education, family disapproval, sexist societies, oppressive governments, jealous husbands, and their own self-doubts—to realize their dreams. The road was not easy for any of them, but these girls didn't give up.

The age qualification made it impossible to include thousands of influential women whose achievements came later in life—incredible women like Sojourner Truth, an African American slave who was a leader in the anti-slavery and women's rights movements; and Valentina Tereshkova, a Soviet astronaut who was the first woman in space. This was especially limiting in the sciences, since many women first had to complete years of study before making contributions to their fields.

As you read the following pages, remember that the girls in this book are just a few of the millions of girls who have done and will do amazing things. We hope their lives will inspire you as they have inspired us. They are definite proof that girls like you can achieve your goals, pursue your passions, and live your dreams. So now it's your turn to go out there and rock the world! After all, in the words of famous girl speaker Anna Elizabeth Dickinson, "The world belongs to those who take it."

Hatshepsut

APPROXIMATELY 1500–1460 BC ⊙ PHARAOH ⊙ EGYPT

[Hatshepsut] had no wish to be remembered merely for
her sex, which she regarded as an irrelevance; she had demanded—
and for a brief time won—the right to be ranked as an equal
amongst the pharaohs.

—JOYCE TYLDESLEY, *HATCHEPSUT: THE FEMALE PHARAOH*

The Egyptians stood shoulder to shoulder, so crowded was the plaza. The sun beat down as they awaited the unveiling of the new royal monument. As the trumpets sounded and the slaves pulled the cloth away from the stone, people in the front rows strained their eyes to get a better look at the carving. What they saw shocked them, and they whispered to those farther back. Within minutes the scandal spread like a wave through the crowd, until everyone knew the surprising details.

In previous monuments, Hatshepsut was shown standing *behind* her husband, fulfilling her role as his queen consort; or standing *beside*

1

Most Egyptians had six or seven children (but almost half died in childhood), and baby girls were just as welcome as baby boys. Popular names had meanings like "Riches Come," "Welcome to You," "Ruler of Her Father," or even "He's a Big Fellow."

━ⅿⅿ━

her stepson, as his guardian and adviser. In this new carving, Hatshepsut stood completely alone. Even more shocking, Hatshepsut was boldly dressed as a man ... in fact, she was dressed as the pharaoh! *What could it mean?* wondered the Egyptians. There had never been a woman pharaoh before. And what about her stepson, who was supposed to be pharaoh? The gods would not be pleased. The *maat*, the ideal state of the universe, would be disturbed.

The girl who would one day become pharaoh was born the eldest daughter to the pharaoh King Tuthmosis I. When her infant sister died, she was raised as his only child. Before Hatshepsut's family came into power, Egypt had been fragmented and often ruled by foreigners. For generations, her royal family had struggled to unite a divided Egypt. Her father eventually achieved this feat, and his reign was a time of great prosperity. He was a beloved and powerful pharaoh to his people.

In order to keep the royal bloodline intact, most royal Egyptians married their siblings. Hatshepsut was no exception. When her father died, young Hatshepsut married her half-brother Tuthmosis II. She was most likely twelve at the time, as most Egyptian girls married around that age. Her brother became pharaoh, and Hatshepsut became his queen consort. She soon gave birth to a daughter, Princess Neferure. Carvings of Hatshepsut during this time show her wearing the clothes of a queen and standing behind her husband.

Many historians argue that Tuthmosis II was a weak and sickly king, and that it was Hatshepsut who secretly ruled. All we know for sure is that Tuthmosis II died when he was still a young man, and Hatshepsut wasted no time increasing her power. Tuthmosis's son from another woman became heir to the throne, as was Egyptian custom. When Hatshepsut was possibly as young as fifteen, she was named guardian to Tuthmosis III, who was about five years old, too young to be pharaoh.

In carvings of this period, Hatshepsut is pictured standing next to her stepson, as she was expected to act as co-ruler until Tuthmosis III was old enough to rule alone. But Hatshepsut had plans of her own.

Although Hatshepsut already held the highest position available to women in Egypt, she wanted more, so she named herself pharaoh— the king! There was a *big* difference between being queen and being pharaoh. The queen was merely the pharaoh's companion. She was not even called by her own name, instead addressed only in relation to the men in her life—"King's Daughter" or "King's Great Wife." A pharaoh, on the other hand, was the unquestionable ruler and owner of all the land and people in Egypt. At any time a pharaoh could ask his subjects to stop their regular jobs and build a giant pyramid or temple. The pharaoh was also responsible for tax collection, food storage for emergencies, construction of canals and buildings, and maintaining law and order. As head of the army, he not only planned military actions but also personally led his troops into battle.

Most important, Egyptians believed their pharaohs were divine: the messengers of the gods here on earth. A pharaoh could speak directly to the gods for his people, helping guarantee prosperity for Egypt and protecting it from disaster. The ancient Egyptians believed that without their pharaoh, they could not survive.

Hatshepsut realized that a female pharaoh would be shocking and upsetting to her people. Egyptians believed in *maat*, the ideal state of the universe, and a female pharaoh was sure to upset the order of things. So, to protect her rule, Hatshepsut transformed herself into something her people would feel more comfortable with. In carvings, Hatshepsut would appear front and center, but flat-chested, dressed in male clothing, and with a fake pharaoh's beard. Her people knew she was still a woman, but these images told them that Hatshepsut could and would serve in a man's role. And since every pharaoh needed a queen consort in order to perform

> Unlike Hatshepsut, Egyptian girls weren't allowed to have jobs outside the home. If they were lucky, they could work as weavers, singers, dancers, or musicians.

3

EGYPTIANS LOVED CATS!

- When a cat died, its owners shaved their eyebrows and tore their clothing to show grief.

- They often mummified their cats—one Egyptian cemetery contained 300,000 cat mummies!

- If you killed a cat, you could be sentenced to death by stoning.

- When royalty hunted, the birds they shot were retrieved by specially trained cats!

many of the ritual duties, Hatshepsut broke another tradition and named her daughter, Neferure, as queen!

It is extraordinary that in Egypt's male-dominated society Hatshepsut's people accepted her as their divine ruler. Even after Tuthmosis III came of age, the Egyptian people kept Hatshepsut as their pharaoh, making her reign last over twenty years! In a time when the average Egyptian lived just thirty years, Hatshepsut's twenty-year rule was astounding.

The territory she commanded stretched from northeastern Africa all the way across the Arabian Peninsula to present-day Syria. Her reign was marked by new and welcome peace, stability, and prosperity. She increased foreign exploration, launching several successful trade missions to lands more distant than Egyptians had ever traveled to before. Hatshepsut is probably most famous, however, for her impressive architectural advances. She worked hard to restore temples that had fallen into decay (even 3,500 years ago, some of Egypt's buildings were already ancient!), and built hundreds of shrines, monuments, and statues. Deir el-Bahri, the mortuary temple on the Nile River she had constructed for her eventual death, is considered one of the most beautiful buildings ever created.

When Hatshepsut grew too old to rule, she finally allowed her fully-grown stepson to become pharaoh. Tuthmosis III followed in his stepmother's well-laid footsteps and became a very popular, successful pharaoh himself. Power must have agreed with Hatshepsut; she died when she was well into her fifties, decades later than the average Egyptian. She was buried in the majestic tomb she had prepared for herself years before. Hatshepsut, a woman who broke all the rules, had a fitting end to her unique life. She was buried in the Valley of the Kings.

Hatshepsut was one of the greatest rulers of ancient Egypt. Her reign was more influential and successful than that of Cleopatra, King Tutankhaman, or Queen Nefertiti, and yet little is known about her today. Why? Years after her death, someone tried to blot out all memory of Hatshepsut. Her statues were smashed to pieces; her image was hacked out of carvings; her paintings were burned; her name was erased from pharaoh lists; her mummy disappeared. A landslide even covered her glorious temple at Deir el-Bahri.

Someone wanted it to look as if Hatshepsut never existed. But who? Her jealous stepson? An angry lover? Later Egyptians who wanted to forget their female pharaoh? This is still a great mystery. In spite of these mysterious and sinister attempts to erase her reign, Hatshepsut's legend could not be buried.

In the late 1800s, archaeologists dug her back to life, discovering her temple and tracing her name underneath newer carvings. They pieced together enough about Hatshepsut to know that she was surely the most influential woman Egypt has ever known. In 2007 her mummy was found and positively identified. Once again, she has claimed her rightful place among Egyptian kings, and the story of Hatshepsut's unconventional life continues to fascinate the archaeologists of today.

HOW WILL YOU ROCK THE WORLD?

I have read all the books on Egypt in the children's library, and I'm now working on the adult library. I'm going to rock the world by becoming an Egyptologist! That's an archaeologist who specializes in ancient Egypt. I will write about my experiences so other people learn more about Egypt and its history. I would also love to open the Sphinx and see what's inside!

KARISSA LIGHT ☼ AGE 13

The TRung SisteRs

APPROXIMATELY 14–43 ◦ WARRIOR QUEENS ◦ VIETNAM

*All the male heroes bowed their
heads in submission. Only the two sisters
proudly stood up to avenge the country.*

—FIFTEENTH-CENTURY VIETNAMESE POEM

From atop the elephants that would carry them into battle, the Trung sisters scanned the crowd below them. Tens of thousands of Vietnamese soldiers looked up at them with pride and fear in their eyes. Fear because they knew that, in the 150 years since the Chinese had invaded Vietnam, no one had risen up against them; the Chinese had more troops, better weapons, and more sophisticated training. But pride, too, because they were fighting for the freedom of their country, and they were led by the greatest heroines the East would ever know. Trung Trac, the older sister, raised her sword and vowed revenge:

Foremost, I will avenge my country,
Second, I will restore the Hung lineage,
Third, I will avenge the death of my husband,
Lastly, I vow that these goals will be accomplished.[2]

With those words, eighty thousand Vietnamese rushed into battle.

These unlikely warrior sisters, Trung Trac and Trung Nhi, were born in a small town in northern Vietnam around 14 AD. Both their father, a powerful Vietnamese lord, and their mother hated the Chinese rulers and weren't afraid to say so. Ever since China had invaded Vietnam in 111 BC, the Chinese had forced the Vietnamese people to pay outrageous taxes and to give up their culture and traditions. The Trung sisters grew up witnessing the harsh and unfair domination of their people. Even though their father died while the girls were very young, they never forgot his dreams for a free Vietnam.

Their mother, Lady Man Thien, was a strong, unusual woman. In traditional Vietnamese society, women had more rights than women of Asia or Europe. They could inherit property and become political leaders, judges, traders, and warriors. But the Chinese rulers were turning back the clock for women in Vietnam, taking away their freedoms. (Have you heard of foot binding?) Lady Thien defied the Chinese when she chose not to remarry, and instead focused all her energy on training her young daughters in the arts of war: military strategy, martial arts, and sword and bow fighting. She knew the battle was coming.

It is most likely that Trung Trac was just a teenager when she fell in love and married Thi Sách, a young district chief. Together with Trung Nhi, they protested Chinese rule and secretly plotted to overthrow the invaders. Trung Trac was described as having "a brave and fearless disposition," and Chinese records claim that Thi Sách

> When the Trung sisters defeated the Chinese in their first battle, Governor To Dinh, who had ordered Trung Trac's husband killed, was so terrified that he disguised himself by shaving off all his hair, and he secretly fled Vietnam.
>
> ~~~~

followed his wife's decisions, not the other way around. It is thought that the teen sisters were in charge of recruiting Vietnamese lords to fight. When the Chinese governor discovered their plan, he brutally executed Trung Trac's husband, hanging his body from the city's gate as a warning to the rebels.

His plan backfired, however. Instead of being cowed, the Trung sisters were so enraged by the murder and growing Chinese injustices that they decided it was time to revolt. They urged their people to be brave and rise up with them. Eighty thousand men and women volunteered for the revolutionary army; most of them were in their twenties! Trung Trac even refused to wear the traditional mourning clothes for her husband so she wouldn't depress the spirits of her fellow warriors.

> The heroism of the women fighters in the Trung army is legendary. In one story, General Phung Thi Chinh led her soldiers into battle even though she was pregnant. She delivered her baby on the battlefield, strapped the infant to her back, and kept fighting.

From the volunteers, the Trung sisters chose thirty-six women, including their elderly mother, to be generals and help them lead the troops. In 40 AD, after 150 years of Chinese rule, the Trung sisters led their people in the first national rebellion against the invaders. The two sisters were a good balance—Trung Trac was a master planner and Trung Nhi a fearless warrior—and with their untrained army, they miraculously succeeded in freeing sixty-five fortresses the Chinese had captured, driving them out of Vietnam. Stories of Trung Trac and her sister spread quickly, until even the leader of China was shaking in his boots. Historical records state, "A woman proudly led a young nation; Even the Han emperor heard of it and was terrified."

After this grand success, the Trung sisters created a new nation that stretched from southern Vietnam all the way into southern China. They were elected co-rulers and quickly reversed many of the unfair policies of the Chinese. They worked to create a simpler government that followed traditional Vietnamese values, and they abolished the hated taxes imposed by the invaders. For the next three years, the Trung sisters ruled their newly independent nation while constantly battling against angry Chinese forces.

Unfortunately, Vietnam's freedom did not last. The Chinese army had more men, weapons, and military experience. In 43 AD, the Trung sisters fought their last battle. Near present-day Hanoi, several thousand Vietnamese soldiers were captured and beheaded by the Chinese, and more than ten thousand were taken prisoner. Rather than surrender and accept defeat, the Trung sisters chose what the Vietnamese consider a more honorable escape: suicide. Some stories say they drowned themselves in a river, while others claim they actually floated up into the clouds.

For the next 950 years, the legend of the Trung sisters encouraged the Vietnamese in their ongoing struggle against the Chinese; many of the rebellions during those dark years were led by women! Their story was passed by word of mouth from one generation to the next until the sisters were actually worshipped as goddesses.

In Vietnam today, there are still constant reminders of the Trung sisters. Stories, poems, songs, plays, posters, monuments, and even postage stamps of the sisters continue to inspire the Vietnamese. In the capital, Ho Chi Minh City, a street is named for them, and many sacred temples have been built in their honor, including the famous Hai Ba ("Two Sisters") pagoda in Hanoi. The Vietnamese government proclaimed them national heroes, and every year, on Hai Ba Trung Day in March, the people of Vietnam celebrate the Trung sisters' sacrifices and courage.

For 150 years, no one in Vietnam had garnered the courage to stand up to the Chinese. Not until the Trung sisters rebelled did the Vietnamese people begin to fight for their freedom. The heroic legends of these brave young women have inspired the Vietnamese people for centuries as they struggled to fight off foreign domination. Soldiers carried pictures of them into battle to give them strength. And, thanks to the Trung sisters, Vietnam now has a long history of famous female warriors. Many people believe that if the Trung sisters had not urged their people to rebel against the Chinese, there would be no Vietnam today.

HOW WILL YOU ROCK THE WORLD?

I will rock the world by being the first female, Jewish president of the United States. Some of the important issues I would take charge of are comparable pay for women and better maternity leave policies.

BASSIE SHUSTERMAN ☼ AGE 14

Joan of Arc

1412–1431 ⚜ WARRIOR AND SAINT ⚜ FRANCE

I was admonished to adopt feminine clothes; I refused, and still refuse. As for other avocations of women, there are plenty of other women to perform them.

—JOAN OF ARC

Arrow and crossbow in hand, young Joan of Arc stood on the fortress tower and looked down into the enemy camp. This courageous seventeen-year-old girl was about to lead the French army into war. She had already won a difficult battle, but she now focused on her final goal: to drive the English away from the French city of Orleans. Joan's heart pounded with fear as she shot a special arrow down into the English camp. Attached to the arrow was a message telling her enemies to surrender the city or she would attack.

The English refused, and Joan once again prepared her troops for battle. The next morning she led an assault against their army. Joan was wounded in the shoulder during the bloody battle, but in the end,

Joan and her men were triumphant. On May 8, 1429, the French army retained control of Orleans due to Joan's brave, inspirational leadership.

Joan was born on a cold January morning in 1412 in the French village of Domremy, where her father worked as a farmer. She was a deeply spiritual girl and had a vision of herself becoming something very different from a traditional peasant woman of that time.

During Joan's childhood, her country was in the midst of the Hundred Years' War with England, and the English army had taken control of much of France. Meanwhile, the king of France, Charles VI, died in 1422. Traditionally, the heir to the throne (also called the "dauphin") would be taken to the city of Rheims to be crowned as the new king. But because of the war, the dauphin could not safely travel to Rheims and thus could not be officially coronated.

When she was about twelve, Joan believed she heard the voice of God telling her that she'd been chosen to accomplish great things. Over the next few years, she had visions of Saint Michael, Saint Catherine, and Saint Margaret, who told her it was her fate to free the city of Orleans (which was on the way to Rheims) and to take the dauphin to be crowned king at Rheims—it was to be a most dangerous mission.

Joan set off to meet her destiny in 1429. As a seventeen-year-old peasant girl, it was quite difficult for young Joan to convince people to help her. But she was an incredibly strong-willed girl with a persuasive personality. To begin her journey, she convinced the captain of the dauphin's forces to furnish her with a horse and a few escorts. Dressed in men's clothing, Joan traveled across war-torn France to meet the future king.

When Joan arrived, the dauphin was skeptical about the young girl's divine mission and military plan, so he summoned a group of clergy and biblical scholars to examine her. Joan conquered their disbelief and was granted her own troops to command in an attack on Orleans. She was even

The children in the village knew all about the war going on around them. Joan and her friends sometimes played in an abandoned castle, pretending to be soldiers in the war.

14

given the rank of captain! The young leader armed herself for battle. She wore a suit of light armor and carried a unique sword with five crosses etched on its blade. She also carried a silk-edged white banner, decorated with an embroidered pattern of Jesus Christ holding the globe in his hands. With her new army behind her, Joan set out for Orleans.

She led a series of successful attacks against the English. Joan's inspirational leadership gave her troops the spirit and morale they needed to beat the English army in the battle. She is described as "most expert in war, as much in carrying the lance as in mustering a force and ordering the ranks, and in laying the guns." The English were defeated, and the first part of Joan's vision had come true.

After her victory in Orleans, which most French people viewed as a miracle, Joan proceeded to the next part of her vision—to take the dauphin to Rheims to be crowned. Once again she had to use her powers of persuasion to convince the dauphin to follow her plan. Joan set off for Rheims, defeating the English in many battles along the way and freeing all the French towns between Orleans and Rheims. The dauphin followed a week later, when he was sure it was safe. He was crowned Charles VII, King of France, in Rheims, uniting France under one leader. Joan stood at his side during the entire coronation.

In 1430 Joan tried to protect France from yet another threat: an attack by the Burgundians. She fought bravely but was captured. The Burgundians sold her to the still-bitter English, who were anxious to take revenge on their female foe. The English brought Joan to trial, accusing her of witchcraft and dressing as a man (which was considered a crime against the Church). The English were afraid of Joan's power and influence over the people of France, and they sentenced her to death without a fair trial.

On May 30, 1431, nineteen-year-old Joan of Arc was burned at the stake. The executioner reportedly said afterward, "I greatly fear that I am damned, for I have burned a holy woman."

Charles VII made no effort to save France's brave warrior, and many believe this was because he was embarrassed that France's victory was won by a peasant girl. Twenty years after Joan's death, Charles VII ordered an investigation of her trial, and the original verdict was annulled. It took almost five hundred years, but finally in 1920 Joan was declared a saint by the Roman Catholic Church.

Joan of Arc's fearless leadership had a substantial influence on the Hundred Years' War. Her military victories demoralized the English and brought new hope to the people of France. Joan's life has inspired countless artists, writers, musicians, and historians. She is the patron saint of France, where her feast day, May 30, is celebrated as a national holiday. Though Joan of Arc lived for only nineteen years, her legacy of heroism has survived for centuries.

ROCK ON![3]

MAYRA AVELLAR NEVES

Mayra Avellar Neves has grown up in one of Brazil's most violent shantytowns, called favelas, outside of Rio de Janeiro. The drug cartels and the police are fighting a civil war that is sometimes so extreme that teachers and doctors can't come into the town. When Mayra was fifteen years old, she organized hundreds of children and teens for a protest march demanding that the violence stop at least during school hours. In 2007 she organized another march, and then in 2008 Mayra won the International Children's Peace Prize, which supported her peace mission with over $100,000.

Sor Juana Inés de la Cruz

1651–1695 ◈ SCHOLAR AND POET ◈ MEXICO

...for there seemed to me no cause for a head to be adorned with hair and naked of learning...

—SOR JUANA INÉS DE LA CRUZ

Fifteen-year-old Juana nervously clamped her hands together as she looked around the room filled with forty of the most intelligent, educated men in Mexico City. She felt like she'd been answering their questions forever. But still, they weren't finished with the exam. The men continued calmly interrogating her, one after another—they asked questions about philosophy, math, history, poetry, religion, and anything else they could think of. For hours she answered their questions. Would she be able to prove her extraordinary intelligence so they would allow her to continue her studies?

Over several hours, she astounded them with her brilliant answers. The stories about her were true after all. Juana's success at the exam was just the beginning of her accomplishments. She later became one

> Although Juana was a better reader than her mother, she kept it a secret. She didn't want to hurt her mother's feelings, and she also hadn't gotten permission to go to classes!
>
> ~~~

of Mexico's foremost intellectuals and also one of its greatest poets!

On November 12, 1651, Juana Ramirez de Asbaje was born in a small hacienda (ranch house) in a Mexican village. At the age of three, Juana began following her sister to school, and she quickly learned to read. She was soon able to read better than her mother. Juana's amazing intellect could not be held back, and she studied anything she could get her hands on, including math, philosophy, religion, literature, history, and the Aztec language. Amazingly, she also learned Latin, a very difficult language, on her own after taking just a few lessons.

When she was seven, Juana heard about the university in Mexico City. Unfortunately, like most other schools at the time, the university accepted only male students. Still, Juana begged her mother to let her dress like a boy so she could attend the school in disguise. Her mother refused, so Juana continued to study on her own from the books in her grandfather's library. She began writing around this time, too, and composed a poem for a religious festival in a nearby town.

When she was nearly ten, Juana moved to Mexico City to live with relatives. Word of her genius spread, and after a few years she was invited to stay with the viceroy (ruler) of Mexico and his wife at their palace. There she continued her studies, entertaining the court with her poetry, songs, and plays. Juana's intellect and abilities became widely respected. When she was fifteen, she faced the extensive oral examination from Mexico's leading intellectuals. She passed with flying colors.

Juana passionately desired to continue learning, but she knew that, as

> Juana was extremely dedicated to her intellectual progress. She even refused to eat cheese because she had heard that it made people stupid (which isn't true, by the way).
>
> ~~~

a girl in Mexico during the 1600s, her role was to be a wife and mother. The only way she could be a scholar was to become a nun. She entered a convent in 1669 and became Sor (Sister) Juana Inés de la Cruz.

> In her lifetime, Sor Juana put together a library that contained 4,000 books—the largest library in Mexico at that time.
>
> ~~~

In the convent, she enjoyed a stimulating cultural life and often entertained the highest members of society as her guests. Best of all, she was able to pursue her studies. She studied science using the best instruments available. The Church sometimes objected to her scientific studies, though, and once she was even asked to stop experimenting for a few months. But even then, Sor Juana couldn't give up science entirely, and she found herself making scientific observations as she performed everyday activities like cooking eggs or looking at the layout of the convent.

Sor Juana wrote poems and plays that were published in Mexico and Spain, devoting much of her writing to the discussion of women's position in society. She argued that women should be given more power and independence.

In 1695 a terrible plague swept through Mexico, and Sor Juana became ill after nursing some of the sisters in her convent. She was unable to overcome this illness and died later that year. Today, Sor Juana lives on in her words and in her example as a brilliant scholar and writer who refused to hide her intelligence or give up her dreams.

Primero Sueño (*First Dream*) is considered one of Sor Juana's most important poems. Its beautiful, symbolic language tells of the awakening of the mind:

> *...so the fantasy was calmly copying*
> *the images of everything,*
> *and the invisible brush was shaping*
> *in the mind's colors, without light*
> *yet beautiful still, the likenesses*
> *not just of all created things*
> *here in this sublunary world, but those as well*

that are the intellect's bright stars,
and as far as in her power lay
the conception of things invisible,
was picturing them ingeniously in herself
and displaying them to the soul.[4]

HOW WILL YOU ROCK THE WORLD?

I will rock the world by writing a book that will open people's eyes. I will interview people living through crises and give them a voice that will reach millions. Writing this book not only gives these people a voice when they never had one but also gives them a chance to be a part of an even bigger movement.

MADDY CENAC   AGE 13

Laura Bassi

1711–1778 ❁ PHYSICIST ❁ ITALY

[Laura] was afraid of no one. [She] fought with clear-sighted determination to win acceptance in the patriarchal world of eighteenth-century science.

—MARTA CAVAZZA, BIOGRAPHER

Mama, Mama, may I please go now?" The embroidery on young Laura's lap was rumpled and frayed. Her mother sighed at Laura's lack of interest. For the hundredth time, she thought that this child should have been born a boy. Reluctantly, she nodded her head; Laura tossed the hated embroidery aside and was off, running to welcome her teacher, who had just arrived for her daily lessons.

Young Laura Maria Caterina Bassi had a thirst to learn. Born in 1711 in Bologna, Italy, at the start of the Age of Enlightenment, she lived in an exciting time, a time of booming curiosity. After centuries fearing the unknown and being terrorized by the mysteries of life, people were beginning to calm down. For the first time, they began to understand

Laura was considered to be an expert in Latin, logic, metaphysics, natural philosophy, algebra, geometry, Greek, and French.

―――

that through observing and questioning the world around them, some of the unknowable could indeed become known. Life was becoming less a terrifying mystery and more an intriguing puzzle to be sorted out.

Unfortunately for Laura, women were not invited to the Age of Enlightenment. Upper-class girls like her were supposed to learn to sew, to manage a home and servants, and to prepare themselves for motherhood. They weren't expected to be interested in or even to have the brains to be curious about the natural world. But Laura didn't let this prejudice stop her. Throughout her life, Laura never settled for what other people wanted of her.

Laura's teacher, a professor at the University of Bologna, was a good one. He was also the Bassi family physician and had agreed, at Laura's father's request, to teach her. He came to the Bassi villa each day. There, in her sunny garden, Laura studied mathematics, philosophy, anatomy, natural history, and languages.

When she was only twenty, her teacher declared she had learned everything he had to teach. It was time for her public examination. He took her to the university to be grilled by the best minds in Bologna. For hours, learned and unbelieving professors, all men, queried Laura about her lessons and challenged her answers.

If you were an enlightened thinker back then, you questioned authority, examined your own motives for prejudice, and relied on your own experiences as the best teacher.

―――

Laura not only gave the right answers, she also defended them with spirit. Despite her sex, they could not dispute her knowledge. So in a solemn ceremony in the Palazzo Pubblico (public palace), she was named a professor of anatomy at the university and a member of the Academy of the Institute for Sciences. In the University of Bologna's six-hundred-year history, no woman had ever been named a professor. Laura was the first.

But, as time went on, it became clear to Laura that, despite her achievements, she was considered special. Not special in a good way—special in that she didn't get to participate in the life of the university like the male professors did. She was a gracious young woman, good at meeting the right people and charming them with her wit and knowledge.

Laura was admired for her good character and charity to the poor, and was sought out by famous thinkers, like Voltaire, when they visited Bologna.

University leaders thought she would make a great figurehead, like a beauty queen of science. They tried to limit her role to hosting parties and welcoming honored guests. She was called the Bologna Minerva, after the ancient Roman goddess of wisdom, invention, and the arts. A lovely title, but Laura didn't want titles. She wanted to teach.

She played along with the game, earning some powerful friends as she performed her hostess duties. Then she went home and quietly did exactly what she wanted. With the support of her husband, physicist Giuseppe Veratti, Laura set up a private teaching laboratory in her home. There, surrounded by her growing family (she eventually had twelve children!), she continued teaching and researching in experimental physics, ignoring the taunts of male scholars who claimed she was neglecting her work to care for her children.

If it bothered Laura, she didn't complain. She kept her head in her studies and in her teaching, and unlike most of her male colleagues, didn't worry about trying to publish her findings or becoming famous. For her, knowledge was the goal.

In 1745, when she was thirty-four, her years of research and her skills at gracefully handling disbelieving colleagues began to pay off. Laura started to get the recognition she deserved. Finally! She was allowed to teach what were known as the male sciences—mechanics, hydrometry, and elasticity. The pope himself, Benedict XIV, nominated her for a post in his Benedictine Academy. But even with the pope's backing, her colleagues still thwarted her and would not allow her to vote, even though she was a member of the academy.

Despite the continuing discrimination, from that time on, Laura's authority was questioned less frequently. She had proved herself and shown that women could do more than manage households. Her fame as a teacher spread, and at sixty-five, two years before her death, Laura was appointed to the prestigious chair of Experimental Physics at the Institute for Sciences in Bologna.

Laura Bassi was an early hero in the fight for women's equality. Her struggle and triumph over male chauvinism are an inspiration to every girl who has been labeled different. As Laura showed, being different can be a wonderful thing.

HOW WILL YOU ROCK THE WORLD?

My dream is to be an author as famous as J. K. Rowling and as funny as Rick Riordan, with more published works than Shakespeare and Ken Follett combined. I could write books with veiled messages, books with relevant themes. I could write stories with strong female characters in a male-dominated historical period. Subtly I could teach people facts through fictional stories. I may be only one girl, but someday I'll be the girl who inspired millions to rock the world.

KATE SAMUELS · AGE 13

Eliza Lucas Pinckney

1722–1793 ✦ AGRICULTURAL ENTREPRENEUR ✦ UNITED STATES

I have the business of 3 plantations to transact,
which requires much writing and more business and fatigue
of other sorts than you can imagine. But least you should
imagine it too burthensom to a girl at my early time of life,
give me leave to assure you I think myself happy...

—ELIZA PINCKNEY

Eliza's father read the letter as the family gathered silently around him. They were all nervous, and Eliza knew it couldn't be good news. With sadness in his eyes, he told them that the military had called him back to his post in Antigua. There was no choice; he would have to leave them alone at their new home in South Carolina. "But who will take care of the plantation?" asked her mother. They all knew that she was too sick to run the plantation without her husband. "I can do it," sixteen-year-old Eliza said quietly. The whole family stared at her when she spoke up.

Eliza was true to her word and soon began her busy days of running the plantation. At five AM, in the pitch dark, it was time to get up. After two hours of reading, Eliza went out to the planting fields to supervise the workers. When the sun finally rose in the east, it was time for breakfast. After that, she spent an hour on music and another hour studying. In addition to her own lessons, Eliza taught reading to her sister and several slave girls from the plantation until dinnertime. After dinner, Eliza devoted several hours to calculating the financial books for the plantations, and then she sewed until dark. Exhausted, she finally went to bed, usually sneaking in a little more time to read or write before she fell asleep.

When little Elizabeth Lucas was born on December 28, 1722, no one knew that she was destined to become one of the great agricultural inventors of history. Born in the West Indies, where her father was stationed as a British army officer, Eliza spent her early years in Antigua before being sent to England for her education. When she was sixteen, her family moved to South Carolina, where her father had inherited a plantation on Wappoo Creek.

A year after the family arrived in America, Eliza's father received the telegram recalling him to Antigua. Her mother was in frail health, so seventeen-year-old Eliza took on the job of running the plantation and overseeing two other family properties. With only her father's letters from Antigua to help her, Eliza ran every aspect of the plantation's business. Like other southern plantations, theirs relied heavily on slave labor. Eliza supervised more than twenty slaves and all the other employees, and she still found time to care for her mother and younger sister.

Eliza's most important contribution to the business came from her experiments with crops during her teen years. Occasionally, her father sent new kinds of seeds from Antigua, and Eliza

> While their plantation used slave labor like all others at that time, Eliza took time out each day to teach several slave girls to read. She hoped they would become schoolmasters for the other slaves' children, who normally received no education.

26

cultivated them in the South Carolina soil. After attempts with crops such as cotton, ginger, and alfalfa, Eliza received some indigo seeds.

Indigo plants are used to make blue dye for fabric and ink. Today, many dyes can be man-made, but in Eliza's time, indigo was in high demand for its unique ability to produce permanent color. English cloth makers depended heavily on indigo and were forced to buy large quantities from France, one of the few indigo-producing countries.

In a few years, Eliza would give French indigo growers some real competition, but not before she suffered her share of setbacks. When she first planted indigo seeds in 1740, nearly the entire crop was ruined by an early frost. Eliza had wisely saved some seeds for the next year, but they yielded only one hundred bushes of the precious plant. Out of this small crop, the plantation produced a modest amount of indigo.

From the West Indies, Eliza's father sent an experienced dye maker, who agreed to help her turn the small indigo crop into finished dye. This is a delicate process, which requires accurate timing and the correct measurement of additives. The dye maker was afraid that if indigo succeeded in South Carolina, it would compete with West Indian indigo, so he deliberately ruined Eliza's tiny crop. He added too much lime to the mix and spoiled the color.

Still determined to make her venture a success, Eliza kept planting indigo seeds. Finally, in 1744, the Wappoo plantation produced a promising crop. Eliza made seventeen pounds of indigo, six of which she shipped to England. The English cloth makers declared her product to be as good as, and even slightly better than, the French indigo they had been using.

Delighted with her success, Eliza shared indigo seeds and taught other plantation owners in South Carolina how to grow it. Soon the new plant was flourishing all over the state; South Carolina had found a profitable new crop for export. In 1747 South Carolina plantations shipped out over 135,000 pounds of indigo, and eventually they exported more than a million pounds annually.

By the age of twenty-one, Eliza's experimental enterprise made her a rich and independent woman. She had already turned down two marriage proposals, but in 1744 she decided to marry Charles Pinckney, a prominent lawyer. They built a mansion in Charleston, but Eliza continued to supervise her family's plantations and pursue her own interests in agriculture and gardening. She experimented with various crops, including flax and hemp. Eliza even tried raising silkworms and producing silk.

Over the course of her marriage, Eliza gave birth to four children. This agricultural pioneer lived to a relatively old age, surviving through the Revolutionary War and the creation of the United States. In 1793 at the age of seventy, Eliza died of cancer. At the time of her death, Eliza's contributions to the American economy were well-known and respected. Her foresight and persistence gave South Carolina a vitally important crop, one which would help support the state's plantations for decades. At her death, President George Washington personally requested that he serve as a pallbearer in Eliza's funeral.

ROCK ON!

WINTER VINECKI

When Winter Vinecki's dad was diagnosed with prostate cancer, the nine-year-old girl quickly realized that there was little awareness of the cancer that stole her dad. She formed Team Winter, a non-profit organization to raise awareness for prostate cancer and to fund prostate cancer research. Unfortunately, her dad passed away only ten months after his diagnosis and never saw Team Winter emerge from its infancy. As a two-time IronKids National Triathalon Champion, Winter raises awareness through her racing and the Winter's Inspirational Talk series, which presents at schools across the United States. Now, athletes around the world race for Team Winter, and Winter has helped raise more than $300,000 for prostate cancer awareness and research, all in honor of her dad.

Phillis Wheatley

1753–1784 ◈ POET ◈ AFRICA AND UNITED STATES

Phillis Wheatley not only belongs squarely in the Black American
literary tradition; she, almost single-handedly, succeeded
in creating that tradition.

—WILLIAM H. ROBINSON, BIOGRAPHER

The terrified young African girl stood on the platform, shivering in front of the white crowd. She had hardly any clothes on, and her bare feet ached. The sights and sounds of Boston harbor were strange and unfamiliar; she longed for her home across the ocean. Alone in the world since she was kidnapped from her family, she looked out at the white faces and wondered sadly whose home she would be going to now. This seven-year-old girl was about to be sold into slavery.

At that time, many families in the American colonies owned slaves to do housework and other tasks. On that summer day in Boston in 1761, Susannah Wheatley set out to buy a slave for her household. Susannah was searching for someone who would be a companion for her, someone who would help fill the void when her own daughter married and left home.

Among the many captured Africans standing before her, Susannah noticed the young, fragile, barefoot girl. She brought the child home, hoping she would work hard at her chores and be someone to talk with. But this young slave was destined for greater things. She was extraordinarily bright and talented, and she would overcome incredible odds to become an internationally famous poet.

Like many African slaves, not much is certain about Phillis's origins. She was probably born in 1753 and may have been from the Fula tribe in western Africa. At the time, slave traders kidnapped African children and brought them to America for sale. Phillis arrived in Boston in 1761 after a long and treacherous voyage across the Atlantic aboard a slave ship. When the Wheatleys purchased her, they gave her the name Phillis and, according to custom, she took their last name as her own.

Phillis shocked everyone with her incredible intelligence. She was able to read English in just sixteen months, and by the age of twelve, she began to study Latin. Phillis loved to read, but her passion was poetry. When she was just fourteen years old, Phillis started to publish her poems.

Luckily, the Wheatleys were supportive of Phillis's creativity. Many slaves were treated harshly, but Phillis was encouraged to read and write whenever she could.

Phillis kept a pen and ink near her bed, and the Wheatleys let her keep a fire burning all night during the winter so she would have a warm room and would be ready to write, should inspiration strike.

As a teenager, Phillis became a celebrity in Boston because of her poetry. She often visited prominent families and held her own in conversations with the most educated people of the city. Phillis definitely enjoyed special privileges, but the fact remained that she was a slave. She still had to deal with the overwhelming racial injustice of the time.

When Phillis was seventeen, she wrote a poem that would bring her world recognition and fame. The poem was for a minister who had recently died, and it was published throughout the American colonies and later in London as well. A few years later, a book of Phillis's poetry was published in London, and Phillis traveled to England for the first time. Phillis was the first African American woman to be published. She was also the first African American author, male or female, to have a book of poetry published.

In 1775, Phillis wrote a poem to honor George Washington, the commander of the American army who would soon become the president of the United States. Her poem ends:

Phillis Wheatley is still inspiring writers today. On the 200th anniversary of the publication of Phillis's book of poetry, African American women poets from around the United States gathered at a festival to celebrate her legacy.

> Proceed, great chief, with virtue on thy side,
> Thy ev'ry action let the goddess guide.
> A crown, a mansion, and a throne that shine,
> With gold unfading, WASHINGTON! be thine.

Washington was very impressed with the poem and invited Phillis to visit him at his headquarters in Cambridge. Just imagine how nervous she must have been! But Phillis swallowed her fear and had a successful half-hour visit with America's most famous leader and his military officers.

By this time, Phillis was free from slavery, having been manumitted (freed) by the Wheatleys soon after her book of poetry was published. Despite the fact that much of Phillis's life was spent as a slave, her poetry often celebrated freedom. Her poems were also about Christianity, and many were elegies for famous people and personal acquaintances. Her success as a poet was remarkable, but when you think about the huge obstacles she faced as a woman, an African, and a slave in Colonial America, her accomplishments become truly extraordinary.

31

HOW WILL YOU ROCK THE WORLD?

My way of rocking the world is with my voice. I will write songs of love and peace and then travel around the world singing and encouraging people to love one another. I will sing to the children of the world and spread the love.

TONYA JOYCE KHAKAZI · AGE 13

Elisabeth Vigée-Le Brun

1755–1842 ◦ PAINTER ◦ FRANCE

I know nothing about painting;
but I have grown to love it through you.

—KING LOUIS XVI, PRAISING ELISABETH'S PORTRAIT OF HIS WIFE, MARIE ANTOINETTE

As the theater darkened, Elisabeth had a moment to look at the audience members around her. She was surrounded by beautiful men and women, dressed in the most sumptuous fabrics, wearing extravagant powdered wigs and sparkling jewels. And among them, there she was, a teenager who had to earn her own living from her paintings! The curtain opened, and she turned her attention to the stage where a young woman was standing before an easel, paintbrushes and palette in hand. Her subject was a beautiful woman wearing a plain muslin dress and a straw hat.

Wait . . . where had she seen this before? To her surprise and delight, Elisabeth realized the actors were playing out a scene from her own life—Elisabeth painting the queen, Marie Antoinette! In the portrait,

33

Elisabeth's most famous portrait of Marie Antoinette was so criticized for the high fee paid to the artist that the royal family had to turn the painting so it faced the wall in the Louvre museum in Paris. It remained that way until after the French Revolution, when it was turned back around.

she had tried to show the queen in a more natural way, instead of her usual elaborate wigs and white face powder, with the result that many people criticized her for painting the queen in her underwear! Not this crowd, thankfully. Elisabeth held back her tears as the entire audience stood up and applauded her. She had never felt so much emotion and pride in her entire life.

Imagine, at fifteen you are such a talented artist that the kings and queens and presidents of the world are begging you to paint them! Elisabeth is still considered one of the most talented and successful portrait painters ever, artist to the richest, most famous Europeans of her time, but Elisabeth Vigée-Le Brun rose from very humble beginnings. She was born in Paris to a middle-class family. Her father was a moderately successful painter and often let his daughter play with his paints and brushes.

From age six to eleven Elisabeth lived in a convent, where she first showed her artistic talents. In her memoirs, she wrote:

During this time I was always sketching, covering every available surface with my drawings; my exercise books . . . had their margins crammed with tiny drawings of heads and profiles. I traced figures . . . on the dormitory walls in charcoal; and as you may well suppose, I was often punished.[5]

After she'd returned home for a year, Elisabeth's beloved father died from swallowing a fish bone. He left the family very little money to live on, so Elisabeth began charging for her paintings. Although she was virtually self-taught, she had such remarkable talent that by age fifteen, she supported her entire family on her wages.

Her reputation spread quickly, and soon the talented teenager was in constant demand to paint the French aristocracy. Meanwhile, Elisabeth's mother remarried a wealthy jeweler. Elisabeth hated the man, who wore her father's clothes, had a terrible temper, and forced her to turn over all her earnings to him. To escape, she rushed into marriage with art collector Jean-Baptiste-Pierre Le Brun, even though her friends warned her, "You would do better to tie a stone around your neck and throw yourself in the river." But she was desperate.

Sadly, her friends were right. Her husband earned no money and forced Elisabeth to give her ample wages to him, which he spent on women, booze, and gambling. Elisabeth was miserable.

> **My only real happiness has been through painting.**
> —ELISABETH VIGÉE-LE BRUN

Fortunately, her art gave her great happiness. In 1778, at twenty-three, Elisabeth was such a celebrity that Marie Antoinette insisted she become an official court painter. Elisabeth wrote of this queen: "I was very much in awe of Her Majesty's imposing air; but she spoke to me in such a kindly fashion that her warm sympathy soon dissolved any such impression."[6] The court appointment turned Elisabeth into the most popular portrait painter. She was sought after by royal families and the most influential leaders of her time, and she earned incredible fees.

For the first time, queens and princesses allowed themselves to be painted in costumes that hid their high social rank. She even set new fashion standards by encouraging her subjects to stop powdering their hair and go natural. The women were delighted to be seen as beautiful. Elisabeth had a talent to see the inner beauty of even the most unattractive person.

But, as time went on, the decadent royal family became less and less popular. So did Elisabeth. Lies were spread

> Elisabeth never finished her final portrait of Catherine the Great. Halfway through her sittings, the queen was murdered by her own son, Paul.

about her: that she charged extravagant fees for her paintings, she threw unbelievably lavish parties, she was having an affair with the minister of finance. Worst of all, Elisabeth's enemies claimed her portraits weren't really hers but were painted by a man!

In 1789 when the French Revolution swept through the country, killing Marie Antoinette, much of the royal family, and their friends, Elisabeth was horrified. She knew that she could be next because of her ties to the queen, so she and her daughter escaped to Italy. They wouldn't see France again for twelve years.

During her exile, Elisabeth traveled all over Europe—Italy, Austria, Czechoslovakia, Germany, Switzerland, England, and Russia. She supported herself and her daughter by painting the royal families and important figures of each country they visited, including another infamous queen, Russia's Catherine the Great.

While traveling, Elisabeth finally broke up with her husband for good. Her letter to him from Moscow shows what an unusual, independent spirit she had:

> *What would I have done without my work? If I had been ill, you would have let me starve; since instead of saving money you have spent it on women who deceived you, you have gambled and lost Monsieur . . . I will neither let my fortune fall into the hands of strangers, since it has been too hard to earn . . . nor will I take advice from anyone.*[7]

At a time when few women supported themselves, Elisabeth chose to be a single mother, earn her own way, and travel the world.

In 1802, after 255 artists petitioned for Elisabeth's return, she was allowed back into France. She continued to paint well into her old age, and in the 1830s, she published her memoirs, which were very popular. In her seventies, she praised her life's work: "This love [of painting] has never diminished. . . . [I] hope that its power will only cease with my life."

Perhaps her art gave her strength and energy as well—she lived to the ripe old age of eighty-seven! During her lifetime she painted over nine hundred paintings, which hang in such prestigious museums as the Louvre in Paris, the Metropolitan Museum of Art in New York, the Uffizi Gallery in Italy, and the National Gallery in London. She is ranked beside such great masters as Raphael and Caravaggio, and was an inspiration to female painters and independent women almost two hundred years before the term feminist was coined.

ROCK ON!

AKIANE KRAMARIK

Daughter of a Lithuanian mother and an American father, Akiane Kramarik began drawing at age four and painting at age six. Now a teenager, Akiane has represented her art on nearly fifty international television shows and sells her paintings for as much as three million dollars. She is also a poet and has written two books, *Akiane: Her Art, Her Life, Her Poetry* and *My Dream Is Bigger than I: Memories of Tomorrow.*

Maria Theresia von Paradis

1759–1824 ⚬ PIANIST AND COMPOSER ⚬ AUSTRIA

*Mademoiselle Paradis is one artist
whom our nation is not able to praise too highly. . . .
This gifted keyboard player is truly astonishing. . . .
More faultless, more precise, more polished
playing is not known.*

—*MERCURE DE FRANCE* NEWSPAPER

Maria Theresia ran her tiny fingers across the keys. She could see nothing, but she could feel their cool, smooth, comforting ivory. When she pressed down on one, out came the most clear and lovely sound. She was entranced. Although she was so young and small that she could barely reach the piano keys, Maria Theresia was drawn to the instrument.

Soon, this young girl would astound audiences around the world and become one of the first famous woman musicians to perform in public. As a blind pianist who played, sang, composed, and taught,

Maria Theresia blazed new paths not only for women but for blind people as well.

Maria Theresia von Paradis was born in Vienna, Austria, in 1759. Her father was the royal court secretary of Empress Maria Theresa, and he named his daughter after her. When she was three years old, Maria Theresia lost her sight. Some believe that her blindness occurred because of an illness, while others claim she was blinded in an accident. As a child, Maria Theresia showed an outstanding talent for music. Unable to read music with her eyes, she had to learn and memorize everything by ear.

She was so gifted that the empress paid for her musical and general education, and Maria Theresia was able to study music with the best teachers available. When she was eleven, she gave her first public performance, singing and playing the organ. By the time she was sixteen, Maria Theresia was recognized as a piano virtuoso and an accomplished singer.

In 1783 Maria Theresia embarked on a three-year concert tour of Europe. She was highly praised wherever she went, but perhaps her most important stop was Paris. Not only did Maria Theresia play fourteen performances there, but she also met Valentin Haüy, who was planning to open the first school for the blind in Europe. Maria Theresia passionately wanted to give other blind people a chance to develop their talents in a time when people with disabilities were often shunned by society. She described to Haüy how she had been taught math, reading, and music. He was then able to use these methods to teach the blind students in his new school.

During her tour, Maria Theresia started composing her own music. She developed a method to set down her compositions by using a peg board. Someone could then transcribe her

Maria Theresia was such an amazing pianist that she inspired other great musicians—famous composers Wolfgang Amadeus Mozart and Franz Joseph Haydn both wrote piano concertos for her, and Antonio Salieri composed an organ concerto for her.

work onto paper. The gifted musician composed at least five operas and three cantatas (compositions for voices and instruments) as well as many other shorter pieces.

In 1808 Maria Theresia started her own music school in Vienna; she wanted to give girls the chance for a good musical education, something that was usually reserved for boys only. Her school taught piano, singing, and music theory to both blind and sighted students. Maria Theresia's school proved to be a huge success, and she continued teaching until her death in 1824. Maria Theresia worked hard to overcome not only her blindness but also the prejudice against women and people with disabilities. During her lifetime she showed the world that there are no limitations to what one girl can achieve.

> One of Maria Theresia's most amazing gifts was her memory. She could play at least 60 piano concertos from memory and could remember all her own compositions, note by note.
> ~~~

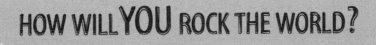

HOW WILL YOU ROCK THE WORLD?

I will be a dancer through high school and college. From there, I will start a small group called Keep on Dancing! for kids or adults to come in and have fun! I will then start a dance company for girls and boys with cancer.

EMILIE KREFT ☀ AGE 13

Sacagawea

APPROXIMATELY 1789–1812
GUIDE AND INTERPRETER ❖ UNITED STATES

*Your woman who accompanied you that long dangerous
and fatigueing rout to the Pacific Ocian and back diserved
a greater reward for her attention and services on that
rout than we had in our power to give her.*

—WILLIAM CLARK, IN A LETTER TO SACAGAWEA'S HUSBAND

There was confusion everywhere. One of the boats was about to capsize! A few men began to bail buckets of water. Another struggled with the rudder, while two men hauled in the sail. They were all in a state of panic. In the midst of this chaos, only one member of the party stayed calm. Sixteen-year-old Sacagawea, with her newborn baby son strapped to her back, quietly balanced herself in the heaving boat.

To the horror of the entire party, some of their precious supplies spilled out into the river and began to float away. They could see food, valuable instruments—and the journals! The only records of their

For the entire journey—
thousands of grueling
miles over mountains and
even down waterfalls—
Sacagawea carried
the infant Pomp in a
cradleboard strapped to
her back.

—⁓⁓—

amazing adventure, written by their leaders, Lewis and Clark, were drifting away in the raging waters. Calm and poised, Sacagawea knew what she had to do. The men in the boat were shocked as they saw the young girl dive overboard with her baby still strapped on her back. Sacagawea rescued almost everything, including the irreplaceable journals.

That day, Sacagawea prevented the loss of crucial cargo, but this was just the beginning of the journey. The young Shoshone girl would continue to prove herself invaluable to the Lewis and Clark expedition as an interpreter, guide, and sign of peace.

Around 1789 Sacagawea was born to a Shoshone tribe in the area that is now Idaho. When she was about eleven years old, she and another Shoshone girl were kidnapped by the Hidatsa Indians, who took Sacagawea hundreds of miles east to North Dakota. There she lived in a Mandan Indian village as a slave. After a few years, she was won by a French Canadian fur trader named Toussaint Charbonneau, who made Sacagawea his wife. When she was only sixteen, she gave birth to their son, whom she named Jean Baptiste but usually called Pomp, which means "leader of men" in the Shoshone language.

In 1804 a team of explorers called the Corps of Discovery, led by Meriwether Lewis and William Clark, arrived in the Mandan villages. President Jefferson had commissioned them to explore the land west of the Mississippi, and they needed guides and an interpreter for the native peoples they would meet. Lewis and Clark hired Charbonneau for the expedition, primarily because Lewis wanted him to bring one of his native wives to help translate for them. The sixteen-year-old Sacagawea packed up her newborn son and prepared to leave the village where she had been kept as a slave. She was heading out west, toward her homeland.

On the long, hard trip, Sacagawea taught the men how to find and cook edible plants so they wouldn't starve when their food supplies ran out, which happened several times. She guided the Corps through Montana and served as the interpreter with the Mandan and Shoshone tribes. Everywhere they went, Sacagawea and Pomp were a sign of peace to the native peoples of the West.

In August 1805 the explorers were desperate to find horses so they could continue their journey. They decided to try to locate Sacagawea's people, the Shoshones, for help. Sacagawea's childhood memories were all they had to guide them. Lewis wrote in his journal:

> The Indian woman recognized the point of a high plain to our right which she informed us was not very distant from the summer retreat of her nation on a river beyond the mountains which runs to the west. . . . She assures us that we shall either find her people on this river or on the river immediately west of it's source . . . it is now all important with us to meet with those people as soon as possible.

They did indeed find the Shoshones a few days later. The Shoshone chief, Cameahwait, welcomed the explorers, and in the midst of the festivities, one of the Shoshone women recognized Sacagawea. She had escaped capture on the day, years ago, when Sacagawea had been kidnapped by the Hidatsas! The two women cried and hugged each other in an emotional reunion.

That afternoon, Lewis called a meeting between the captains of the exploration party and the chiefs of the tribe. Sacagawea was to translate to Chief Cameahwait. No sooner had they started the meeting than Sacagawea jumped to her feet and ran to embrace the chief, who had seemed very familiar to her. Chief Cameahwait was Sacagawea's brother!

The expedition party stayed as guests of the Shoshones for a month, and when they left, Chief Cameahwait

Legend has it that the Nez Perce tribe planned to kill the entire Lewis and Clark expedition, but Sacagawea persuaded them that the expedition was peaceful. If they had been a war party, she pointed out, they would not have taken along a girl and her baby.

—⁓—

gave them food, horses, and detailed instructions for their passage across the Rocky Mountains. The group successfully reached the Pacific Ocean, and the end of their exploration, in November 1805. They weathered a rainy winter in hastily built cabins before they began their return trip back to St. Louis in late March 1806.

Sacagawea, Charbonneau, and Pomp started back with the expedition but went their own way before the group arrived in St. Louis. Little is known of what happened to Sacagawea after this. Some accounts say that in her early twenties she had a daughter, Lizette, and probably died in 1812, soon after the birth. Other accounts, however, claim that Sacagawea returned west to join the Shoshones and lived to be almost one hundred years old.

Sacagawea's bravery has been immortalized by numerous memorials and historical markers across America. Lakes, mountains, rivers, state parks, and Girl Scout camps have been named after her. She's even featured on one-dollar gold coins! Her life has become a legend of courage and adventure.

ROCK ON!

MARJORIE TAHBONE

Helping the community and fellow Native Americans is highly important for Marjorie Tahbone. When she was in high school, Marjorie advocated through Native youth organizations, conferences, and student council. Then she started racking up awards, including Miss Arctic Native Brotherhood, Miss World Eskimo-Indian Olympics, and Miss Indian World. Her world title keeps her busy traveling all over North America as she acts as an ambassador for the continent's more than five hundred Native nations. Marjorie is of Inupiaq Eskimo and Kiowa Indian descent and attends the University of Alaska in Fairbanks.

MARY ANNING

1799–1847 ◦ FOSSIL HUNTER ◦ ENGLAND

It was fossils like the ones Mary discovered
that scientists relied on the most in helping them
to decipher the global geologic record.

—SHELLEY EMLING, BIOGRAPHER

Eleven-year-old Mary gathered her hammer and chisel and set out for the high cliffs along the coast. The night before, there had been a violent storm with strong winds and droves of rain. She knew the water had washed away layers of dirt, uncovering shells and fossils. With any luck, she'd be able to find a few unique specimens to sell to tourists as curiosities.

As Mary walked along the beach, she noticed something strange. Lying near one of the cliffs were some objects that appeared to be large bones. Intrigued, she immediately went to get a closer look. Mary began chiseling away the rock near the bones, and the more she uncovered, the more excited she became. In front of her was a huge skeleton, unlike anything she'd ever seen. With its long tail, short flippers, and sharp teeth, it looked like a sea dragon!

What Mary had *really* found was one of the first and most complete skeletons of an Ichthyosaurus, or "fish lizard," a dinosaur that lived about two hundred million years ago. This thrilling childhood discovery inspired her to spend the rest of her life hunting for fossil remains, an occupation that would bring her fame and respect in the world of science.

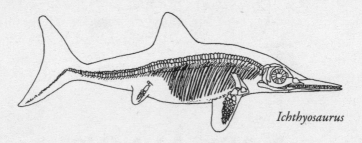

Ichthyosaurus

Mary Ann Anning was born in 1799 in Lyme Regis, a town on the southern coast of England. Her father was a carpenter who collected and sold fossils as a hobby. He often took Mary and her brother to search the coast for shells, sea dollars, and other interesting items. Tourists loved the coiled fossil shells that the Annings sold. At the time no one knew exactly what these were, but it would later be discovered that they were the fossil remains of ammonites, prehistoric mollusks that lived during the time of the dinosaurs.

When her father died in 1810, eleven-year-old Mary and her family decided to continue selling fossils. She found her first dinosaur skeleton just a few months later. She hired some quarrymen to extract it from the rock and then sold the skeleton to a man who bought things for museums. Mary's creature was later named Ichthyosaurus.

After this first discovery, Mary continued with her business, always searching for new fossils. When she was in her early twenties, she discovered a second dinosaur skeleton. This one was called a Plesiosaurus, or "near lizard," because of its long, thin body and its four elongated flippers that looked almost like legs. A few years later, Mary found the skeleton of a birdlike dinosaur, the first ever to be found in England, which was later named Pterodactyl, or "wing finger."

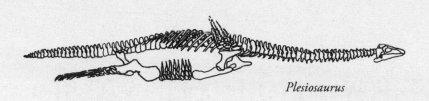

Plesiosaurus

For the remainder of her life, Mary continued hunting and selling fossils. Mostly, she sold the small fossilized shells to tourists, but her dinosaur skeletons attracted the attention of wealthier and more scholarly customers as well. Over the course of her career, she found other ichthyosaurs and plesiosaurs, which brought high prices from scientists and collectors and increased the world's knowledge about these ancient creatures.

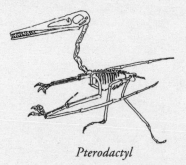

Pterodactyl

By the time she died in 1847, Mary had become well-known for her discoveries. As a prehistoric-fossil hunter, she helped found a new area of study. And as one of the earliest professional female scientists, she opened new doors for women.

HOW WILL YOU ROCK THE WORLD?

There have always been environmental problems accumulating around the world: endangered animals, pollution, deforestation, overpopulation . . . all of which connect so deeply with each other that it is hard to untangle and find a solution to them. However, there are so many ways to help: planting trees, raising money to help save forests and create shelters for animals, protesting against poaching, going green, not littering. If I'm going to rock this world, I know exactly how to . . . by saving our environment!

ADELINE LEFEVRE ☼ AGE 13

The BRONTë SisteRs

1816–1855 (CHARLOTTE), 1818–1848 (EMILY), 1820–1849 (ANNE)
AUTHORS ◉ ENGLAND

No coward soul is mine
No trembler in the world's storm-troubled sphere
I see heaven's glories shine
And Faith shines equal arming me from Fear.

— A POEM BY EMILY BRONTë, FROM THE SISTERS' FIRST PUBLISHED BOOK

There was a quiet knock at the bedroom door. Charlotte and Emily, who were already tucked in and reading by lantern light, looked up from their books with surprise. Who could it be so late at night? Their wild brother Branwell burst into the room. "Look what Papa has brought me!" he cried, handing them a small box. They opened the lid, and to their delight, they found a whole troop of brightly painted, wooden soldiers!

Charlotte grabbed one from the box and proclaimed, "This shall be the duke!" Emily took another tiny soldier, crying, "This one shall

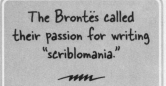
The Brontës called their passion for writing "scriblomania."

be mine. He is rather grave looking, so let us call him Gravey!" Their youngest sister, Anne, heard the commotion from her room and came running. She, too, chose a soldier for herself, which they named Waiting Boy. A thousand stories swirled in their heads: dragons, castles, grand adventures, and great dangers. At that moment the three sisters began creating the magical world of Gondal. All alone in their spooky, lonely house, they dreamed of becoming famous writers.

The girlhood dreams of the Brontë sisters came true beyond their wildest fantasies, but at a high cost. All three sisters published successful novels that became classics of literature, and they were sensational stars in their day. Yet their world was overshadowed by tragedy and unhappiness.

The three famous Brontë sisters, Charlotte, Emily, and Anne, originally came from a family of six children. They had two older sisters, Maria and Elizabeth, and a brother, Branwell. Just after baby Anne was born, the family moved to Haworth, a cold, wet, industrial town in northern England, where their father, the Reverend Patrick Brontë, had gotten a job. Behind their new house were the wild and windy moors, and in front stood the church and the cemetery. Their windows looked out over a sea of gravestones—perhaps a sign of the sorrows to come.

Haworth had no sewers and the water was very polluted, so it wasn't surprising that almost half the children born there died before turning six and the average age of death in town was just twenty-five years old. Soon after the Brontës moved there, their mother died. The children were left in the care of their eccentric father. Mr. Brontë loved his children and taught them literature, history, and geography; he held weekly discussions on politics, poetry, and literature. But he also kept them isolated from the rest of the town.

Fortunately, the children had their books, their imaginations, and most important of all, their pens. Charlotte wrote: "The liveliest pleasure we had . . . lay in attempts at literary composition." They entertained themselves by writing poems, stories, and even a monthly magazine. Their lonely house, the graveyard, the mysterious moors—all worked their way into the sisters' writing.

But Mr. Brontë began worrying about the sisters' futures. He realized that their only career option would be teaching. For that, they would need more education. When he sent Maria, Charlotte, Elizabeth, and Emily off to a boarding school, he had no idea of the nightmare he had committed them to. The girls were tormented by the terrible food, bitter cold, cruel teachers, and boring lessons. Worse yet, in 1825 a tuberculosis epidemic swept through the unsanitary school, and Maria (age eleven) and Elizabeth (age ten) died within months of each other. Charlotte and Emily were devastated and returned to the safety of their home.

Once again, the girls studied around the kitchen table. In 1826, when Branwell received his toy soldiers, the children began creating a world of stories around them. For the next five years, the girls—who were ten, eight, and six—wrote their tales in tiny, handmade books that were just two inches tall (exactly the right size for the toy soldiers!), in teeny-tiny handwriting that only they could read. In one year alone, they wrote eighteen of their tiny books!

Like the characters in her books, Charlotte was strong-willed. At twelve she vowed never to marry, so she could devote her life to writing, and at fourteen she had already written twenty-two manuscripts! After a few more years at a new school, where she blossomed into a star student, Charlotte returned home at sixteen to teach her younger siblings and to continue writing.

When she began showing her work to people outside her family, the reviews were not encouraging. She wrote to Robert Southey, a famous poet, asking for advice and enclosing some poems. He wrote back, "Literature cannot be the business of a woman's life, and it ought not to be." But Charlotte refused to let this sexist attitude discourage her—she wrote sixty more poems that year. She turned down all marriage proposals to write. Her younger sisters were inspired and started to take their own writing more seriously too.

While struggling to get published, the girls had to work as teachers and

Charlotte caused a scandal when she exposed the crimes of her childhood school in her novel JANE EYRE.

The popular Brontë
stories have been
made into movies.
Check 'em out!
mmm

governesses. They hated it. In 1845 Charlotte read some of her sisters' poetry. It was fantastic! She convinced them they should publish a book of verse together. They paid to have the book published, but had to call themselves Currer, Ellis, and Acton Bell to avoid the prejudice against women writers. It didn't do them much good, however. Although the book got great reviews, it sold only two copies!

Undaunted, they turned their energy back to their stories, working together and reading their tales aloud to each other. Out of this collaboration came Emily's *Wuthering Heights*, Anne's *Agnes Grey*, and Charlotte's *The Professor*. The three novels were sent off to various publishers, again using the male names, and after a year of waiting, *Wuthering Heights* and *Agnes Grey* were accepted for publication. *The Professor* was rejected everywhere.

Again, Charlotte refused to be discouraged by other people's opinions, and she immediately started another novel. From her own experiences, Charlotte crafted *Jane Eyre*, the story of a rebellious governess who refuses to accept her station in life. When her manuscript reached the publishing offices of Smith, Elder & Co., it was passed around to several editors. They all loved it. One of the owners, George Smith, took it home with him; he couldn't put it down and read the entire five-hundred-page novel in one sitting! Charlotte would finally be a published writer like her sisters.

Jane Eyre was an instant hit, praised for its original voice and fascinating story. It was also strongly criticized. People at that time weren't used to strong, passionate heroines, attacks on church hypocrisy, or the idea of equal rights for all people, regardless of their class or sex.

Wuthering Heights was equally controversial for Emily's descriptions of passionate love. When it first came out, it wasn't as successful as *Jane Eyre*, but it eventually became one of the most popular novels of all time. One critic describes it as "perhaps the most passionately original novel of the English language."

Agnes Grey was well-received, but Anne's second book, *The Tenant of Wildfell Hall*, was a controversy. It was a feminist story, attacking marriage laws and the different rules that men and women had to obey. Critics were so alarmed that they cautioned young ladies not to read any of the books written by the "Bell brothers."

As praise and criticism for these revolutionary books grew, so did curiosity about the authors. The public wondered if they were really men, or if the novels were actually written by just one person. To quell the growing rumors, Charlotte and Anne went to London in 1848 and met with their publishers face-to-face for the first time. George Smith was amazed that such powerful novels came from the minds of these petite, quiet, shy young women. When the news got out, the Brontë sisters became even more of a sensation than before.

They had made it! But real life for the Brontës took a turn for the worse. Their brother, who was never successful, drank heavily and abused drugs. Like his sisters before him, he caught tuberculosis and died in September 1848. By December, Emily had also contracted the illness, and she died at age thirty. Just when Charlotte thought she could endure no more heartache, her baby sister Anne caught the same deadly disease and died the following spring, at just twenty-eight years old. In less than a year, Charlotte had lost her three remaining siblings and was left alone with her father. Of this time, she wrote in a letter to a friend, "Why life is so blank, brief and bitter, I do not know."

For the next six years, Charlotte cared for her father, taking pleasure only from her writing. She published two more popular novels, *Shirley* and *Villette*, but felt something was missing from her life. In 1854 Arthur Nicholls, a man she had already rejected, asked Charlotte again to be his wife. She wasn't exactly in love with him, but she knew he was kind and had a great sense of humor—something she could use after all her tragedy.

She said yes, and in June of 1854 they were married. In just a few months she grew to love her husband deeply and was happier than she'd ever

> Some people believe that the Brontë's drinking water was tainted, since it flowed beneath the graveyard next door, and that this was the reason for their sicknesses and early deaths.

been in her life. Then at the age of thirty-nine, she became pregnant. But again, her happiness was not to last long. A few months later she and the baby died from complications.

Three lonely sisters, with little formal education, cooped up in a strange house on the remote moors, published three of the most thrilling novels of the day. While their novels were considered strange, brutish, feminist, and revolutionary one hundred fifty years ago, today they are loved as some of the most powerful, groundbreaking stories of all time. Along with Shakespeare, Chaucer, and Dickens, the names of these sisters—Charlotte, Emily, and Anne—have gone down in history as three of the most talented authors ever.

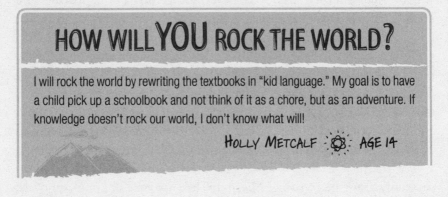

HOW WILL YOU ROCK THE WORLD?

I will rock the world by rewriting the textbooks in "kid language." My goal is to have a child pick up a schoolbook and not think of it as a chore, but as an adventure. If knowledge doesn't rock our world, I don't know what will!

HOLLY METCALF · AGE 14

FloRence Nightingale

1820–1910 ◦ NURSE ◦ ENGLAND

What a comfort it was to see her pass ... We lay there by the hundreds; but we could kiss her shadow as it fell and lay our heads on the pillow again, content.

—A WOUNDED SOLDIER PRAISING THE LADY WITH THE LAMP

Florence walked down the dark hall of the British hospital. The floors and walls were disgusting; they looked like they'd never seen a good scrubbing. And what was that foul smell? When she turned a corner, Florence could see a stream of blood and human waste flowing down the middle of the hall and emptying into an open drain. She plugged her nose, covered her mouth, and continued on.

She could hear horrible cries and moans through each doorway, and when she peeked her head into a room, she saw a filthy man lying in a bed that looked like it hadn't been changed for weeks.

The poor soul was being tormented by a cloud of flies attracted to the stench. Florence was horrified. "Nurse, nurse!" she cried. And when the so-called nurse finally staggered into the room, she could see that this woman was no nurse at all—and she was drunk! Florence couldn't believe her eyes. It was no wonder so many people died in hospitals! Everywhere she looked, she saw things that could be improved, but no one seemed to care. These were just poor people, after all.

But Florence cared. She dedicated her life not only to comforting the sick but also to reforming hospitals and the profession of nursing. She completely reinvented the way hospitals were run and how the sick were cared for. The kindhearted Lady with the Lamp, as she was called, became a legend in her own time and is now recognized as the founder of modern nursing.

Florence and her older sister were educated at home in England by their father. While Florence was an intelligent student, she was also quite pretty, and her parents expected her to make a good marriage. Florence, however, had other plans. Even as a young girl, she felt the life of a wealthy English woman was boring and pointless. She wanted to do something meaningful. In 1837 the rebellious sixteen-year-old heard the voice of God speak to her, calling her to do good works. At the time, she wasn't sure exactly what "good works" she should do, but she began visiting the sick in local villages, bringing them food and changing their bedding.

Her parents disapproved. It was unladylike, they said. When Florence asked to visit hospitals to learn more about nursing, her parents were horrified! Hospitals were for poor people who couldn't afford to be cared for at home—certainly no place for a beautiful, wealthy bride-to-be. Florence defied her parents and followed her calling.

Indeed, English hospitals were worse than Florence had ever imagined. The nurses were uneducated, poorly paid, and often drunk. It's not surprising that they neglected patients and treated them cruelly. Diseases spread quickly in the filthy, overcrowded rooms. In fact, at the time, anyone who actually went into a hospital could expect to die, rather than to get better. Florence began studying the problems, writing to experts around the world, and formulating her own ideas for improvements.

As a girl, Florence loved animals and had a pet owl named Athena.

58

During this busy time in her life, Florence was also being pursued by one of the most eligible bachelors in England, Richard Milnes. She actually cared strongly for Richard and even wanted to marry him, but she knew that it would destroy her chances of pursuing a nursing career. When Florence finally rejected him and vowed never to marry, she became quite depressed.

To help cheer her up and at the same time distract her from her nursing passion, Florence's parents sent her off to tour Europe. Instead of changing her mind, however, the trip actually strengthened Florence's resolve. She studied how the sick were cared for in Italy, Egypt, Greece, and finally in Germany, where she visited an innovative hospital and nursing school. She saw that when patients were clean, well-fed, and taken care of, they recovered more quickly.

> Florence was an inventor. She created systems for pumping hot water into patients' rooms, lifting food from kitchens to nursing floors on small elevators called dumbwaiters, and giving patients special bells they could ring to call a nurse to their room. These are still used in hospitals today.

When Florence returned to England, she shocked her parents by packing up and moving out. She went back to the German nursing school, where she trained for four months, then finished up her studies in Paris, where exciting discoveries were being made about germs and how disease is spread. By 1853 thirty-three-year-old Florence was appointed superintendent of a women's hospital in London, where she was able to put her theories into practice. Florence's improvements were very successful, and her reputation grew. Her dreams were finally coming true!

In 1854 England entered the Crimean War (in present-day Turkey) and suffered heavy casualties. When newspapers reported on the terrible medical facilities for wounded soldiers, it caused an uproar in England. The government recruited Florence to go to the battle area and try to improve conditions. She took thirty-eight nurses and set off for the front lines of the war.

Conditions were far worse than the papers had reported. They arrived at a war hospital in Turkey to find thousands of soldiers lying on

The United States
Army consulted
Florence on how to care
for sick and wounded
soldiers during the
Civil War.

straw in the hallways, covered in their own blood and excrement. Everything was crawling with fleas and rats. There were no beds, soap, blankets, or clean clothing, not even enough water for the injured men. At night the injured and dying men were left alone in the terrifying darkness.

To Florence's surprise, the army officers were not happy to see the nurses—they resented women telling them what to do. So Florence did the work without their help. There were no funds for supplies, so Florence used her own money. They cleaned the hospital and the men, and even brought in a sanitary team to drain the cesspool that the hospital was built on. They set up a kitchen and made sure the wounded soldiers were well-fed. They comforted the men by reading to them and writing their letters home.

Each night Florence lit her lantern and made her rounds, giving comfort and advice to the frightened men. When they saw her light coming down the hall, the men instantly felt that everything would be OK. The grateful soldiers began calling her the Lady with the Lamp.

Miraculously, the death rate at the hospital dropped from 42 percent to 2 percent in just five months! Florence's renovation of the hospital complete, she turned her attention to improving the entire army medical system. She sent plans back to England for reorganizing all military hospitals, keeping military medical records, and establishing an army medical school to train doctors and nurses in techniques and medicines specific to the battlefield.

When the war ended in 1856 and Florence returned home, she was a hero. She was such a success that the public raised money for Florence to continue her reforms in the hospitals of England. She was invited to meet with Queen Victoria to discuss further improvements. The queen set up a Royal Commission to decide on Florence's suggestions, and before long, England had its first Army Medical School, greatly improved army barracks and hospitals, and the best army medical records in Europe.

Sadly, either the mental or physical strain of the war seemed to have ruined Florence's health. Four months after returning to England, she hid herself away, never appearing or speaking in public again. In fact, for much of the next fifty years, Florence didn't even leave her bed. But this didn't stop her from working.

She continued to campaign for improved health standards around the world, publishing over two hundred books and reports. In 1860 her book, *Notes on Nursing*, was first published. Since then it has sold millions of copies, been translated into dozens of languages, and is still in print today.

> Some people think Florence suffered from post-traumatic stress disorder after the Crimean War, and this is what kept her bedridden for the rest of her life. PTSD is now an accepted mental disorder, which usually affects soldiers who have been exposed to trauma during a war.

That same year, Florence used the money raised by the public to found the Nightingale Training School of Nurses in London—the only school of its kind in the world. Graduates of the school went to work in British hospitals and abroad, establishing the Nightingale Model worldwide.

For the rest of her long life (she lived to be ninety!), Florence was sought after by governments all over the world for her advice on nursing, hospitals, and sanitation. Her farsighted reforms changed the very nature of modern healthcare and saved countless lives. Even today, the Lady with the Lamp continues to inspire nurses, doctors, and healthcare workers around the world.

ROCK ON!

AMY CHYAO

Sixteen-year-old Amy Chyao beamed when US President Barack Obama recognized her for her advancements to medicine. Amy helped to tailor photodynamic therapy, the use of light and nanoparticles already used to attack skin cancer cells, for other cancers within the body. This work won her first place at the Intel International Science and Engineering Fair and earned her a trip to the White House. Amy has also won other science awards for working to reduce traffic's environmental impact and is a national spelling bee finalist.

HaRRiet Tubman

1820–1913 ❖ ABOLITIONIST ❖ UNITED STATES

*There was one of two things I had a right to, liberty or death;
if I could not have one, I would have the other; for no man
should take me alive; I should fight for my liberty as long as
my strength lasted.*

—HARRIET TUBMAN

Harriet stood in the hot sun, shucking corn with the rest of the slaves. Out of the corner of her eye, she noticed a tall black man slip into the woods. Her heart raced! Was he running away? Harriet had always dreamed of running away. Worry gnawed at her heart—would he make it? Kicking up a cloud of dust, the overseer galloped past, pulling out his snakeskin whip as he neared the woods. He was after the slave! She had to do something, but what? What could a fifteen-year-old black girl do to stop a white man?

Without thinking, Harriet took off after them. She caught up at the plantation store, where the overseer had ahold of the slave. Harriet

Harriet's bravery should
come as no surprise—her
parents were of the
Ashanti people. These
fierce warriors lived
in West Africa, where
they successfully fought
off British invasions
during the 1800s.

—mm—

recognized the terror in his eyes. When the overseer spotted her, he yelled, "You. Hold this man while I tie him for his lashing." In a quiet, angry voice, Harriet replied, "No, I won't." He was so stunned by her words that he lost his grip on the slave, who bolted from the store. Before you could blink, Harriet moved so she stood in the door, blocking the white man from chasing the slave. In his rage, the overseer grabbed a lead weight and hurled it toward the escaping slave, but he missed. The weight hit young Harriet right between the eyes. Blood gushed from the wound, and the world went dark.

It was the first time this fifteen-year-old girl helped one of her people run toward freedom and took the beating for it, but it certainly was not her last. In just a few years, Harriet would have a new name; one that would be praised by blacks and feared by white slave owners—Moses, after the Jewish hero who led his people out of slavery in Egypt. Harriet "Moses" Tubman would lead more blacks out of slavery than any other person—male or female, black or white—in American history.

Oh go down, Moses,
Way down in Egypt land,
Tell old Pharaoh,
Let my people go.
—A SONG HARRIET SANG AS SHE LED SLAVES TO FREEDOM

Harriet was born into slavery sometime in 1820 (no one bothered to keep track of slaves' birthdays), on a plantation in Maryland, one of eleven children of Harriet Green and Benjamin Ross. Her parents, who couldn't marry because it was illegal for slaves then, were brought to the plantation from Africa in chains. Her mother worked in what they called the big house, and her father cut wood for their white master, Mr. Brodas.

Brodas made much of his fortune from renting out his slaves and also from breeding and selling them, like animals. As a young girl, Harriet saw many of her siblings and friends "sold down the river," never to be seen again. It was her worst nightmare: to be sold to another plantation farther south, far from her parents and friends. Harriet always dreamed of running away to the North, where she would be free.

Slaves didn't get to be kids for long. When Harriet was just five, her master rented her out to work for a local family. She slept on the kitchen floor and shared scraps with the dog for meals! Harriet hated working inside, near her white captors, so she convinced her master that she worked better outdoors. When he witnessed her unusual strength, Brodas quickly put her to work with the men, plowing, chopping wood, and driving oxen. Harriet considered the hard labor an improvement, but she never lost sight of her dreams of freedom.

But getting to freedom was no easy thing. When a master reported a runaway slave, groups of white trackers searched the surrounding countryside with dogs. If caught, a runaway would be whipped, branded with the letter R (like cattle!) for "runaway," and sent to the dreaded Deep South, where treatment of slaves was even more horrific. But Harriet's back was already crisscrossed with scars from her many whippings. She wasn't afraid.

Harriet first helped a runaway slave when she was just fifteen, and the blow she took from the overseer almost killed her. She was in a coma for weeks, and it would be over six months before she could walk again. For the rest of her life, she was scarred by an ugly dent in her forehead and suffered what were called sleeping fits. Several times a day, no matter where she was or what she was doing, Harriet would suddenly drop into a deep sleep from which no one could wake her until she regained consciousness on her own. In spite of her wounds, Harriet never regretted her act of rebellion.

Harriet's first escape attempt occurred when she was seven. She got caught sneaking a sugar cube from her master's house, but before they could whip her, she ran to the pigpen and hid inside for five days. Starving, she fought piglets for scraps from the trough.

Once Harriet and her passengers hid in a pile of manure, breathing through straws!

Her master, however, was not pleased, and decided it was time to sell his troublesome slave. Even while Harriet was lying in a coma, he brought prospective buyers in to look at her. As she recovered, Harriet prayed, "Oh dear Lord, change that man's heart . . . " When that appeal didn't work, she switched tactics, "Lord, if you're never going to change that man's heart, *kill him . . .* " Soon after she made her pleas, Mr. Brodas fell ill and died.

But his successor still planned to sell Harriet, so she got ready to escape even though by then she was married and her husband strongly discouraged her. She'd heard tales of the Underground Railroad—a network of people willing to hide runaway slaves in their homes and help them as they journeyed north to freedom. By night, slaves walked and hid in wagons, boats, and trains. By day, they slept in safe stations —houses, churches, and barns whose owners supported freedom for blacks. Harriet could read a compass and planned to use the Railroad to make it to the Free States.

One dark night in 1849, Harriet finally set out alone. At the first station she was given slips of paper, called tickets, with names of friendly families up the road. At these houses, Harriet presented her tickets and was allowed in. At one house they gave her a broom and told her to sweep the porch. She was upset until she realized that this was their way of hiding her—no one would question a black woman sweeping. Traveling by night, Harriet trudged through ninety miles of swamp and woods until she finally crossed into free Pennsylvania. Of her first taste of liberty, she said, "I looked at my hands to see if I was the same person now that I was free. There was such a glory over everything; the sun came like gold through the trees, and over the fields, and I felt like I was in heaven."[8]

But Harriet wasn't satisfied with her own freedom for long. She worried about her family, friends, and others still living in bondage. She immediately began planning her first rescue mission. From 1850 to 1860, she made nineteen risky trips back into the South, conducting three hundred runaway slaves north to freedom.

Harriet always gave herself a head start on the whites. She arrived at plantations late Saturday night, disguised as an old woman, and then led groups out on Sunday, knowing owners wouldn't chase them that day. She was also remarkably cool-headed on those long, treacherous journeys north and discouraged fear in her passengers. If any runaways got scared and wanted to turn back (which would endanger the entire Underground Railroad), Harriet put her pistol to their head and said, "Move or die." It worked. In ten years, Harriet never lost a single passenger.

Harriet even snuck back to the Brodas plantation, where her chances of being recognized and caught were terribly high. By 1857 she had rescued her entire family, including her elderly parents. By then Harriet's husband was remarried, so she left him behind for good.

At first Harriet led her escaped slaves to the northern states of America, but this became too dangerous when Congress passed the Fugitive Slave Law in 1850, demanding the return of escaped slaves and punishing those who helped them. Harriet refused to give up and instead led her people all the way to Canada. It turned a ninety-mile escape route into a five-hundred-mile one, but at least the ex-slaves knew they would be truly free.

The mysterious thief angered and scared white plantation owners, who just assumed that Moses was a man. How could a woman—a black woman, at that—be so cunning and bold as to steal slaves right from under their noses? The usual reward for catching a slave ranged from a hundred to a thousand dollars, but slave owners put an amazing reward on Moses's head: *forty thousand dollars*! Though the South swarmed with bounty hunters, they never caught Harriet as she freed slave after slave.

When the Civil War broke out in 1860, many southern slaves fled their masters and ran to the Union troops, who unfortunately weren't prepared to deal with them. Harriet heard what was

The queen of England was so impressed with Harriet that she sent her a medal and invited her to come to England. Harriet didn't go, but she reread the queen's letter so often it "was worn to a shadow."

happening and traveled from her home in Canada to South Carolina, where she worked as a nurse on the front lines, caring for both black freedmen and white soldiers.

Harriet was soon recruited as a spy because of her extensive knowledge of the southern states and her legendary courage. She led groups of black soldiers into enemy territory while informing Union officers about the actions of Confederate troops and the locations of ammunition depots and slaves waiting to be freed. Union General Rufus Saxton praised her: "She made many a raid inside the enemy's lines, displaying remarkable courage, zeal, and fidelity." In one legendary raid, Harriet and 150 black soldiers attacked a Confederate outpost in South Carolina and freed 750 slaves! What sweet revenge for Harriet and her men.

After the war, Harriet settled in Auburn, New York, a former station on the Underground Railroad, to care for her elderly parents. Never one to miss out on any excitement, in 1870 fifty-year-old Harriet fell in love again—this time to a man in his twenties! She married Nelson Davis, a Civil War veteran, and became a popular and moving speaker on the rights of blacks and women.

Despite her fame and all she'd accomplished, Harriet was practically penniless after the war. She and friends wrote letters asking the US Government to pay her a pension, just like it paid to male soldiers who had served in the Civil War. No luck. When her husband died at forty-four (yes, Harriet outlived her young husband!), the government paid her an eight-dollar monthly pension as his widow, but it still didn't recognize her for her own service!

Harriet's dream in her old age was to build a home for sick and elderly ex-slaves, a place where they would be safe and taken care of after all their struggles. She earned money by selling copies of her biography and was finally able to build her retirement home in 1908. At age eighty-eight, she was one of the first to move in. Five years later, surrounded by her friends and family, and in the home she'd built, Harriet finally quit the struggle and died of pneumonia at the age of ninety-three.

In Cambridge, Maryland, not far from where Harriet lived in slavery, Tubman Street reminds us of the girl who refused to accept her lot in life. When up against the foreboding wall of slavery, the woman they called Moses persevered, risking her life again and again to help others and to lead her people to freedom.

HOW WILL YOU ROCK THE WORLD?

I would rock the world by ending racism, violence, world hunger, and global warming. We can change the world because together we can make a difference. Life is beautiful, so let's make peace!

ODALYS GONZALEZ PRADO ⚛ AGE 12

MaRgaRet KNight

1838–1914 ❖ INVENTOR ❖ UNITED STATES

*I sighed sometimes, because I was not like other girls;
but wisely concluded that I couldn't help it, and sought
further consolation from my tools.*

—MARGARET KNIGHT

The whirring and clicking of the machines hummed in Margaret's ears, almost hypnotizing her as she worked. Suddenly, the loom next to hers began making strange noises and, before she could react, it went haywire! The heavy spindle flew off, and its steel-tipped needle plunged into her neighbor's leg. Margaret stared in shock—blood was everywhere. The mill erupted in chaos that didn't stop until the screaming girl was carted off to the hospital. When things calmed down and people went fearfully back to work, Margaret couldn't get the image out of her mind. There had to be a way to automatically shut off a loom when it malfunctioned so the spindle wouldn't fly off and injure the worker. But how?

It's a wonder that twelve-year-old Margaret ever solved this riddle. She lived in a time when a woman was more likely to sprout wings than become an inventor. Victorian girls were raised to be good wives and mothers, nothing more. They were taught to bake, sew, and clean house rather than work with tools and other so-called manly interests. And yet, from her earliest memories, Margaret was obsessed with tools, machines, and how to build things. She described her unpopular interests:

As a child, I never cared for things that girls usually do; dolls never possessed any charms for me. I couldn't see the sense of coddling bits of porcelain with senseless faces: the only things I wanted were a jack-knife, a gimlet, and pieces of wood.[9]

Margaret's girlfriends in Springfield, Massachusetts, were appalled and called her a tomboy and worse. But she didn't let them stop her creativity. The boys liked her just fine, and they came around constantly begging her to make things for them. She was famous in the neighborhood for the kites and sleds she built. She took a lot more pride in those than she did in her household chores.

Margaret's family was poor, so she didn't get much schooling and had to work in a cotton mill when she was young. But it was her work there that gave twelve-year-old Margaret the inspiration for her first invention. After the mill accident, she was consumed day and night until she figured out a way to shut off a malfunctioning loom. Her stop-motion device was immediately put to work at the cotton mill and then in mills all over America. A twelve-year-old's invention saved countless lives.

Margaret didn't earn any money for this invention, and she spent her teen years working in various mills, in photography and engraving studios, and even repairing houses. This didn't leave much time for inventing, but Margaret constantly

At the paper bag company, Margaret and other women were paid a third less than men doing the same jobs because the owners thought a woman couldn't take care of the machines!

—mm—

studied the tools and machinery she worked with, learning how they functioned and imagining how she might improve them. It was during these years that her inventions took shape in her head.

Her most famous invention came to her while working at the Columbia Paper Bag Company. At the time, paper bags had to be glued together by hand. They were envelope-shaped and flimsy, usually falling apart before people could get their groceries home.

Americans recycle more than a billion paper grocery bags every year! These bags are made from a kind of paper called Kraft, a German word meaning "strength." You can reuse them many times.

Margaret devised a machine that could cut, fold, and paste the bags together without human labor. The bags it made were strong and flat-bottomed, like our grocery bags today.

She made thousands of trial bags on a wooden model before deciding to patent her invention. A patent is a document that proves a person invented something, and it would give Margaret the right to sell her idea or let others use it for a fee. Patents are how inventors make money for their ideas. Although Margaret had been inventing her entire life, she was thirty years old when she applied for her first patent. She knew her wooden model wouldn't do for the patent office, so she took it to a shop to have an iron one built. When it was finished and she applied for her patent, Margaret got the shock of her life.

A certain Charles Annan beat her to it. He'd already applied for a patent on a bag-making machine that looked just like hers! It turns out he'd studied her model while it was in the shop. Even though he admitted to spying, Annan claimed that he had the idea first and that no woman could possibly understand the mechanical complexities of such a machine. Margaret was outraged.

Although she knew it would be an uphill battle to fight male prejudice, she had put too much work into her invention to just give up. She scraped together all her money and paid a lawyer one hundred dollars a day to help her fight for what was hers. They called witnesses—her boss at the bag factory, the machinist who built her iron model, her

73

roommate—who all testified that Margaret had been working on the machine years before Annan.

Margaret herself defended her mechanical abilities, "I have from my earliest recollection been connected in some way with machinery." She showed the court early sketches, notes, and photos, and she even let the judge read her diary, which was full of dreams about her precious bag machine! The judge and jury were overwhelmed with evidence that Margaret was no average lady. She won her case and her patent.

Victory was sweet, not just because Margaret had proved that a woman could invent an incredibly complex machine, but also because it was worth a fortune! She got her machines built and formed the Eastern Paper Bag Company to produce her bags. And unlike many inventors, Margaret enjoyed the fruits of her inventing success *during* her lifetime. Her invention earned her extraordinary attention (it could do the work of thirty people!), around fifty thousand dollars, and a medal from Queen Victoria!

Even though Margaret had little schooling, she taught herself everything she needed to know about patent law, contract negotiating, and licensing. It was a good thing too, because over the next forty-five years, she came up with almost ninety more inventions. She patented about twenty-five of them, including new shoe-cutting machines, window sashes, rotary engines, and motors for cars. She spent almost every day in what she called her experiment rooms until she died at seventy-six. In the last year of her life, a *New York Times* article described her continued creativity and stamina: "Miss Margaret Knight . . . is working twenty hours a day on her eighty-ninth invention."

Margaret was one of the most productive female inventors ever. Her fame made her a role model for other female inventors to follow in her footsteps. She was not only a brilliant inventor but also a shrewd businesswoman and a real fighter when it came to protecting her ideas. Margaret never let people's prejudices about women stop her from doing what she loved—figuring out ways to make things better—and she never let anyone else take credit for her ideas! In 2006 she was inducted into the National Inventors Hall of Fame.

ROCK ON!

LI BOYNTON

Li Boynton has been an inventor since she was in the fifth grade, when she developed a machine to take salt out of seawater so it would be drinkable. Then when she was a junior in high school, she invented a method of testing water for contaminants by using glowing bacteria. This process is very inexpensive and will benefit the world's developing nations. Li hopes to reduce the number of people who die from contaminated water every year.

Anna Elizabeth Dickinson

1842–1932 ✦ ORATOR, ABOLITIONIST, AND SUFFRAGETTE
UNITED STATES

[Anna] dressed as she desired; she traveled where and how she
willed; she delivered lectures on subjects many people felt should not
even be mentioned in the presence of unmarried young ladies.

—GIRAUD CHESTER, BIOGRAPHER

The young speaker stood in front of more than eight hundred people. It was Anna's first major speech, and she was understandably nervous. Some of the people in the audience seemed to be looking at her with doubt, as if they were saying to themselves, "How could this teenage girl tell us anything we don't already know?" As she began her speech, "The Rights and Wrongs of Women," Anna's large eyes scanned the audience. Her knowledge of the subject was so thorough that she needed very few notes. With each word she spoke, eighteen-year-old Anna felt more confident. The skepticism was quickly fading from the faces in the audience.

Anna passionately expressed her views, arguing that women should be allowed to vote and to hold any job they wanted. At the time, women in the United States were not allowed to vote, and many professions—like being a doctor or a lawyer—were off-limits to them. Anna's opinions were radical for the time, but her clear voice and dramatic style impressed everyone in the audience. After two hours of speaking, Anna stepped down from the platform amid loud applause. She had just begun a career that would make her one of the most famous and influential women of her time.

Anna Elizabeth Dickinson was born on October 28, 1842, in Philadelphia, Pennsylvania. It was a time in the United States when tensions were high. Slavery was a hotly debated issue: should it be legal in all states, some states, or should it be outlawed altogether? Anna was the youngest of five children born into an abolitionist family which fought to outlaw slavery. She was raised with the belief that slavery was morally wrong, and she was involved in the anti-slavery movement from a very young age. When she was just thirteen, she even wrote an article for an anti-slavery newspaper.

Anna attended school until she was fifteen years old, when she had to start working to help support her family. She held various jobs in publishing houses, law firms, and schools. When she was seventeen, Anna attended a meeting on women's rights. This young girl spoke up, expressing her views that women should be given the same opportunities as men. Her speaking ability was so impressive that she was soon asked to contribute to other debates on women's rights and slavery.

> Anna's childhood home was actually a station on the Underground Railroad, a secret organization that helped slaves escape to freedom.

> During her tours across the country, Anna enjoyed mountain climbing. She climbed many of the highest peaks in Colorado—at a time when women were considered too frail for exercise!

Anna gave her first major speech at the age of eighteen, and her successful career as an inspiring speaker had begun. She toured the country, gaining the respect of revolutionary leaders such as abolitionist William Lloyd Garrison and women's rights activists Susan B. Anthony and Lucretia Mott.

In 1863 Anna was asked to become a campaign speaker. She began delivering powerful speeches in support of the Republican candidate for governor in New Hampshire. When the candidate won, Anna's persuasive speeches were hailed as a major reason. Her success led many politicians to invite Anna to be their campaign speaker in elections, and her fame as an orator continued to grow.

Perhaps her most important speaking engagement occurred in 1864 when Anna was formally invited to speak in front of Congress. She was the first woman ever to speak before the House of Representatives! After this speech she was introduced to President Lincoln, for whom she later campaigned when he was up for reelection.

Between her campaign speeches, Anna continued to speak out about the evils of slavery, a topic that grew more

> Anna was often compared to the brave French heroine Joan of Arc, who was the subject of one of her most popular speeches.

and more controversial as the nation moved toward war. During the Civil War, the United States fought over her cause, the abolition of slavery, and Anna was undoubtedly the most famous female speaker in the country. At the war's end, her powerful words were acted upon—the slaves were freed.

Anna traveled the country delivering more speeches on controversial topics. She knew that she couldn't shy away from subjects just because they weren't popular. The world needed her message. Only through open debate could these problems be solved. So Anna dared to stand up for what she believed, even when there were many who disagreed with her. Her obvious independence, courage, and passion shocked many people but earned her the respect of a great many others.

Here's an excerpt from one of Anna's speeches:

Give to every child in America a spelling book and a free schoolroom, and to every intelligent and respectable person, black and white, man and woman, a ballot and freedom of government, and you will see that this country will stand stronger and stronger amidst the ruins of dissolving empires and falling thrones.[10]

Anna worked to promote racial and political equality for all. At the National Union Convention in 1866, she joined Theodore Tilton and Frederick Douglass in developing an idea for an amendment to the US Constitution. The amendment would outlaw discrimination based on "race, sex, color, or previous condition of servitude." Their proposal was accepted by the Republicans and became the fifteenth amendment to the Constitution. Unfortunately, the word *sex* was omitted from the final amendment, and inequality between men and women was not outlawed.

> Anna never married, although she had at least three offers.

Anna's career paved the way for other female activists and strong women. In the 1870s, she retired from public speaking to begin writing and acting in plays. Anna lived to be ninety years old and even performed in the theater as well. But this outspoken woman will always be remembered for her fame and influence as one of the greatest speakers the United States has ever known.

HOW WILL YOU ROCK THE WORLD?

The dire circumstances faced by impoverished children around the globe is an issue that is very close to my heart. At my suggestion, my family is currently sponsoring several children in India so that they may have a chance at education to break the chain of poverty. I hope to work as a doctor overseas in countries with very poor medical care systems. I want to be a very active citizen in my city, my country, and my world.

JULIA GOYAL · AGE 17

Sarah Bernhardt

1844–1923 ◎ ACTRESS ◎ FRANCE

*It is not at all necessary to be handsome or to be pretty; all that
is needful is charm, the charm that holds the attention of the
spectator, so that he listens rapt, and on leaving seeks to be alone,
in order to recapture the charm he has felt.*

—SARAH BERNHARDT

The curtains pulled back, and light flooded the stage. Sarah squinted out at the audience and could barely make out the faces of the experienced actresses and actors who had come to judge her performance. She was ready—she had practiced and practiced the scene for her entrance exam at the prestigious French theater company. The judges stopped her. "You need to choose a boy to act in the scene with you," they said. Sarah was horrified. She had rehearsed the scene alone. She didn't even *know* any of these boys. How could she concentrate on her lines with some boy messing up her scene? "I won't," she told them.

The judges were shocked at her stubbornness but offered to let her choose another piece instead. But she hadn't practiced anything else.

What scene would she do now? Then it struck her—she would tell them a story. She chose a fable she knew and began to recite it. Again, the judges were bewildered—it was a very odd choice—but after the first few lines, the panel was captured by her clear, melodious voice. Before she could even finish, she had been accepted. Thirteen-year-old Sarah had become a member of the Conservatoire of the Comédie-Française. It was the beginning of a long path that would lead her to become known as the Divine Sarah and the greatest actress of all time.

> Sarah was always known as a rebellious and dramatic girl. She was even suspended three times from her convent school.
>
> —*mm*—

Sarah Bernhardt was born Rosine Bernard on October 22, 1844, in Paris. Sarah's mother was a Jewish woman from Holland who was known for her beauty and her love of travel. Sarah never knew her father. While her mother traveled around Europe, Sarah was cared for by family and friends. At twelve, she entered a convent school and a few years later decided she wanted to become a nun and teach at the school.

Sarah's family, however, wasn't sure that she should make such an important decision when she was only fourteen years old. A family friend suggested that she study acting at the Conservatoire of the Comédie-Française, a prestigious French theater. After her unusual but brilliant entrance performance, Sarah was accepted into the acting school.

> LE PASSANT was so highly acclaimed that Napoleon III himself asked for a command performance in his palace garden.
>
> —*mm*—

Sarah studied at the Conservatoire for a few years and then performed at the Comédie-Française. She made her first stage appearance when she was seventeen, but she received mixed reviews. After two more disappointing performances and a violent argument with a lead actress, Sarah left the company. She continued to act over the next few years and even tried her hand at singing, despite being tone-deaf.

Sarah didn't give up. She signed with another theater company and trained intensively. Her acting received consistent good reviews, and she developed a loyal following of fans. Her big break came in 1869, when she played a page in a play called *Le Passant*, which ran for more than one hundred nights in Paris. Sarah was on her way to a long-lasting and triumphant career, during which she came to be called the Divine Sarah.

The tragedies of the next few years interrupted Sarah's path to success, however. First a fire in her Paris apartment destroyed everything she owned. Then the Franco-Prussian War began, and Paris was under attack. During the siege, Sarah created a hospital in the theater where she performed.

After the war ended in 1871, Sarah returned to the stage. She was praised for her role in *Ruy Blas*, which was written and directed by famous author Victor Hugo. Her energy and emotion were riveting, and she delivered her

> Offstage, Sara was known to be quite eccentric. She had many exotic pets, including a lion and a monkey. She also had a special coffin made, which she slept in.
> ⟶

lines with entrancing poeticism. Her performance was so well-received that she was invited once again to act at the Comédie-Française. There, Sarah enjoyed success after success, firmly establishing her place as a leading actress.

Sarah loved to take on challenging roles. One controversial performance was in *L'Aiglon*. All of Paris's most prominent citizens turned out to see fifty-six-year-old Sarah portray a young man. This groundbreaking actress was one of the very first to play male roles, an idea that shocked many people. Proving the skeptics wrong, Sarah delivered a superb performance as Napoleon's illegitimate son and as other male characters. In other performances, Sarah played Cleopatra, Joan of Arc, Queen Elizabeth, Hamlet, Saint Teresa of Avila, and many more roles.

After achieving great fame in France, Sarah became an international star, touring Europe as well as North and South America. She began producing plays and even bought her own theater, which she named the Theatre Sarah Bernhardt. Sarah's passion for theater was unconquerable. When she was seventy-one, her leg had to be amputated due to an injury, but she refused to give up acting. Instead, she reworked all her scenes so she could remain seated throughout the plays. Sarah continued acting until she was seventy-eight years old!

> Sarah had many rocky love affairs. She once married an aspiring actor, only to separate from him a few months later.

After acting in hundreds of plays and earning international fame, Sarah died in Paris in 1923. The world mourned the loss of a legendary actress, who was arguably the greatest of all time. Sarah was one of the first true international celebrities in the theater. Her performances and her life were the very definition of stardom.

HOW WILL YOU ROCK THE WORLD?

I will rock the world by writing screenplays. I would like to make people laugh when I write something funny and cry when I write something sad. Even if I just make one person feel better by watching my movies, I'll know I did well.

MAUREEN GUALTIERI ⚙ AGE 12

Edmonia Lewis

1845–1907 ✦ SCULPTOR ✦ UNITED STATES AND ITALY

She found a path virtually
uncharted by African Americans,
that of an artist.

—KIRSTEN PAI BUICK, BIOGRAPHER

Thwack! The heavy hammer smacked down on the point chisel, and a hunk of marble crashed to the ground. *Thwack!* Another piece fell. *Thwack!* And another. Edmonia Lewis stood back and looked at the stone that remained. *It's time*, she thought. With a smaller chisel and hammer, she began tapping at the roughed-out block. *Tink. Tink. Tink.* Dust flew as Edmonia chipped away, slowly revealing the face of one of her heroes.

I don't care what they say, Edmonia thought as she worked the stone. *I can do this.* She glanced at a photograph of Colonel Robert Gould Shaw and remembered watching him lead his regiment of black soldiers through the streets of Boston a few months back. They were on their way to fight in the Civil War, to fight against the slavery of her people. Edmonia was proud to see so many black soldiers, and even prouder to see twenty-one men she recognized from her own college.

But now Colonel Shaw was dead, along with most of his troops. They were killed six weeks after the parade, charging Fort Wagner in South Carolina. Edmonia was determined to carve Shaw to honor his sacrifice and the bravery of his men. Her white artist friends didn't think she was ready, but Edmonia knew she was.

What Edmonia didn't know was this sculpture would soon pay her way to Italy, where she would study with master sculptors and create art that would be known around the world—an unheard-of triumph for a half-African American, half-Native American, eighteen-year-old girl growing up in the time of slavery.

Edmonia Lewis had a most unusual childhood. She was born near Albany, New York, in 1845. Her father was a free black man, and her mother a Chippewa Indian famous for her talent as a moccasin maker. Edmonia described her early years as nomadic: "Mother often left her home, and wandered with her people, whose habits she could not forget, and thus we her children were brought up in the same wild manner. Until I was twelve years old I led this wandering life, fishing and swimming . . . and making moccasins."

Edmonia's parents died when she was nine years old, so she moved in with her mother's Chippewa family in the Niagara Falls area. The family earned money making and selling Native American souvenirs to the tourists there. At that time, the Niagara River, which forms the border between the United States and Canada, was a popular crossing point for black slaves escaping to Canada (where slavery was illegal). Edmonia grew up watching slaves race for freedom *and* slave owners chase them down. She and her family had to be careful not to be mistaken for fugitive slaves—that kind of mix-up could get them shot, or kidnapped and forced into slavery. Witnessing this life-or-death struggle would inspire Edmonia's later artwork.

> Edmonia's Chippewa name meant "Wildfire."

Sunrise, Edmonia's brother, didn't stay in New York after his parents died. He headed for the Wild West, where a gold rush was underway. He must have done well for himself because he paid for Edmonia to go to school. In the north at that time, blacks could attend abolitionist schools, run by white people who opposed slavery. Edmonia started at New York Central College and later, when she was fourteen, moved on to Oberlin College in Ohio.

Oberlin was a center of the abolitionist movement in America. The school was deeply religious, and its founders believed it was a sin to own

> Edmonia said of her HAGAR sculpture: "I have a strong sympathy for all women who have struggled and suffered." She sold the piece for $6,000—nearly a million dollars in today's money!
>
> - 〜〜〜〜 -

another human being. Teachers and students there fought to end slavery, and it was also one of the few schools in the country to accept black and female students. It was at Oberlin that Edmonia first discovered her talent for drawing. There, her passion for art was born.

Oberlin was also the setting for a great tragedy in Edmonia's life. In January 1862 two of Edmonia's white friends fell seriously ill after a sleigh ride with two young men. They accused Edmonia—whom they claimed served them hot spiced wine before the ride—of trying to poison them. Edmonia was arrested.

While awaiting her trial, a second tragedy struck. Edmonia was seized from her home at Oberlin, dragged to a field behind the house, beaten to unconsciousness, and left for dead in the winter snow. Luckily, some students and faculty noticed she was missing and searched the area until they found her. Edmonia was so injured that her trial had to be postponed while she recovered. When the case was finally heard, Edmonia was still so weak that two people had to help her into the room. Her case was dismissed due to a lack of evidence and motive—but the damage was done. White people at the school and in town were suspicious of Edmonia. It's likely that Edmonia was suspicious of them as well.

In the months following the scandal, Edmonia endured taunting from classmates and accusations of several more petty crimes, which were also dismissed without evidence. Just before the end of her final year at Oberlin, Edmonia was forced to leave the college without graduating.

Was Edmonia guilty, or did the girls lay blame for their drinking on someone likely to be suspected by the community? We'll never know. But we do know these events changed the course of Edmonia's life. Although she never spoke publicly about the accusations, she did say, "I thought of returning to [the] wild life again." But her passion for sculpture and her determination to prove Oberlin was wrong about her won out. Instead of returning to her family in Niagara, eighteen-year-old Edmonia set off for Boston to become a sculptor.

There she studied under Edward A. Brackett, a well-known sculptor, and sold her first piece, a sculpture of a child's foot, for eight dollars. After that first sale, she hung a sign on her studio door that read: "Edmonia Lewis, Artist." She was on her way.

Neoclassical was the popular style of the time, wherein artists copied the themes and look of ancient Greek sculpture. Edmonia soon mastered this approach, but the subjects she chose were uniquely her own. One of her earliest pieces was a plaster medallion of the revolutionary abolitionist John Brown, who led an antislavery revolt in Virginia in 1859.

Soon after came her bust of Colonel Robert Shaw, leader of the all-black 54th Regiment of the Civil War. After seeing Shaw in a parade, Edmonia asked a white friend who knew his family for photos to work from. The friend refused. She didn't think Edmonia was a good enough sculptor and told her so. Edmonia didn't let that stop her, however, just as she hadn't let the poisoning scandal stop her. She found photos on her own and carved the bust anyway. When she showed the sculpture of Shaw to his family, they liked it and gave Edmonia permission to sell copies. To the surprise of her doubters, she sold nearly one hundred copies at a fundraiser to equalize pay for black soldiers.

THE DEATH OF CLEOPATRA was lost for many years. It was first bought and placed at a racetrack near Chicago. Over the years, the racetrack changed into a golf course, then a munitions plant, then a post office, but the statue remained even though people didn't remember what it was.

Finally, in 1987, the statue was identified and restored by a Chicago historical society.

88

She gave a portion of her proceeds to the cause and used the rest to travel to Italy, the heart of the sculpting world.

In Italy, Edmonia's talent and success grew. She studied with Hiram Powers, the top American carver at the time, learning how to enlarge her clay sculptures into life-sized marble statues. The themes of Edmonia's sculptures were unusual for her time, inspired by her unusual life: *Forever Free* showed an African American in broken chains, celebrating the end of slavery; her *Bust of Henry Wadsworth Longfellow* was in honor of his poem "The Song of Hiawatha," which changed white feelings about Native Americans; Hagar, depicting the biblical slave who was banished to the wilderness, was likely inspired by Edmonia's own experiences at Oberlin; and *The Old Indian Arrowmaker and His Daughter* reflected the clothing and decorations of the Chippewa tribe Edmonia grew up with.

One of her later sculptures, *The Death of Cleopatra*, was a hit at the 1876 Centennial Exposition in Philadelphia due to its unique depiction of Cleopatra *after* death, a shocking, controversial choice at the time. Critics praised it, even the critics at Oberlin, who ironically wrote: "The renowned sculptor . . . Miss Lewis took her first lessons in art at Oberlin about 16 years ago." It seems Edmonia had proved herself at last.

The unlikely sculptress spent the rest of her life in Italy, where she enjoyed fame and financial success and avoided much of the racism of America. Life in America had seemed stacked against her: she was half-black, half-Native American, and a woman during a time when none of those groups had many rights or opportunities. Yet Edmonia triumphed over the prejudices of her time, overcame poverty, and prevailed over a scandal that might have ruined her. Edmonia would not give up on her dreams—she was the first African American and Native American woman to gain international fame as a sculptor, and she blazed a trail for women and minority artists who followed after her.

HOW WILL YOU ROCK THE WORLD?

I will rock the world by becoming a wildlife photographer, and with all that I make from doing that, I will establish a wild animal rescue center. I'll make many contributions to organizations that help protect endangered species. Hopefully I can help save many wild animals from abuse and also teach people just how much we need animals in our world in order for us to survive.

MACKENZIE PAGE · AGE 15

Emma Lazarus

1849–1887 ❖ POET ❖ UNITED STATES

*Until we are all free,
we are none of us free.*

—EMMA LAZARUS

Fourteen-year-old Emma sat alone in her room. She was bored with her music and language studies and thought she'd try something new. She dipped her pen in ink and began to capture on paper the words that floated in her mind. The more she wrote, the more difficult it got. She had no practice with meter or rhyme, and the whole endeavor was a struggle. After hours of work and many sheets of crumpled paper, Emma was ready to give up on writing poetry. But something inside her told her to keep trying. Something wanted her to put those beautiful words on paper, so she kept going. Years later her hard work would pay off.

On July 22, 1849, Emma Lazarus was born into a Jewish family in New York City. From an early age, Emma was interested in reading and

Emma didn't just write about the social causes she believed in—she took action. She visited the main immigration camps and helped new Jewish immigrants adapt to life in New York. She also helped found the Hebrew Technical Institute, providing much-needed education for the new immigrants.

writing. In addition to common school subjects, private tutors taught her music; European literature; American poetry; and foreign languages like German, French, and Italian. Emma began writing her own poetry when she was about fourteen years old.

Her talent with words was so great that her first volume of poetry was published when she was just seventeen years old. She went on to write a novel, a play, and many more poems and magazine essays. She soon became a well-known, respected American author.

Emma was inspired by nature, music, and art, but she was especially moved by social issues. In the 1880s, Jews in Eastern Europe were facing horrible discrimination and persecution. As thousands of Jews immigrated to New York in order to escape, Emma became aware of their struggles, and she began writing poems that dealt with Jewish persecution through history. She also wrote a play about medieval persecution of Jews, and she translated medieval Jewish poems. She collected these poems and the play into *Songs of a Semite*, which was published in 1882.

After her death, Emma received a great honor when her poem "The New Colossus" was engraved on the podium of the Statue of Liberty. Her words would now welcome all immigrants who sailed to the United States in hope of a safe haven from persecution. Today, her poetry still greets immigrants, even if they arrive in New York by airplane instead of ship. The last few lines of Emma's poem are now inscribed on the wall of the reception hall in the John F. Kennedy International Airport.

THE NEW COLOSSUS

Not like the brazen giant of Greek fame,
With conquering limbs astride from land to land;

Here at our sea-washed, sunset gates shall stand
A mighty woman with a torch, whose flame
Is the imprisoned lightning, and her name
Mother of Exiles. From her beacon-hand
Glows world-wide welcome; her mild eyes command
The air-bridged harbor that twin cities frame.
"Keep, ancient lands, your storied pomp!" cries she
With silent lips. "Give me your tired, your poor,
Your huddled masses yearning to breathe free,
The wretched refuse of your teeming shore.
Send these, the homeless, tempest-tost to me,
I lift my lamp beside the golden door!"[11]

ROCK ON!

NONI CARTER

When Noni Carter was twelve years old, she started writing a short story about her ancestors' experience of slavery in the American South. The short story grew into a three-hundred page novel, *Good Fortune*, which Noni worked on for six years to revise and polish. At eighteen, her hard work paid off when her book was published by Simon & Schuster. The book won the Parents' Choice Gold Award, and Noni continues to inspire and educate youth around the country.

Helen Keller

1880–1968 ❧ WRITER AND ADVOCATE ❧ UNITED STATES

I long to accomplish a great and noble task, but it is my chief duty to accomplish small tasks as if they were great and noble.

—HELEN KELLER

Six-year-old Helen stood near the water pump and held one hand under a stream of rushing water. With her other hand, she felt the movements of her teacher's hand as Anne used sign language to spell out *w-a-t-e-r*. Blind and deaf, Helen had spent most of her childhood unable to communicate with anyone around her. Because she could not hear, she had forgotten that objects had names; she had forgotten the concept of language. But now, here at the water pump, it was all coming back to her. She finally understood! This coldness that she washed her hands in every day was water. *What are the names for everything else?* she wondered excitedly. *What is my name?*

With Anne's help, Helen took her first step toward learning to communicate. Eventually, Anne would help Helen overcome her disabilities,

The most difficult subject for Helen was math, but she loved to read and write—and her autobiography was published when she was just 22!

teaching her to read, write, and even speak. Helen's triumph changed attitudes toward disability; she taught the world that people with disabilities may face unique challenges, but can make extraordinary contributions to society.

Helen Keller was born on June 27, 1880, in Tuscumbia, Alabama. She was a bright child who could walk and speak a few words before her first birthday. But tragedy struck when Helen became ill at nineteen months. This illness left her blind and deaf, and for the next five years, Helen lived in a dark, silent world. Like any other little girl, she had toys and liked to play. She especially liked dolls, and her favorite was one she named Nancy. But Helen had a fitful temper, and she sometimes beat her beloved doll only to hug it lovingly a few minutes later.

Such behavior worried Helen's parents, but they had no way to communicate with their child. They taught her a few easy signs, like nodding her head yes and shaking it no and pretending to cut a piece of bread to show that she was hungry. She could also perform some everyday tasks like folding and putting away clothes. But the Kellers worried that their daughter would never learn the difference between right and wrong and that they would never be able to tame her violent temper.

When Helen was six years old, the Kellers hired Anne Sullivan as her teacher. Anne, herself, was barely twenty years old when she arrived, and she had overcome her own difficulties. As a fourteen-year-old orphan, she entered the Perkins Institute for the Blind. Anne was legally blind and could not read, but she learned quickly at the school. A series of operations almost fully restored her eyesight, but her personal experience with blindness motivated her to help other blind children.

Now Anne faced the difficult task of teaching Helen. For the first couple of weeks, she gave Helen objects and then spelled their names into her hands. But Helen didn't associate the objects with the words until the day at the water pump. From that day forward, Helen made rapid progress. By the end of the summer, she had learned 625 words. Over the next few years, she learned to read braille, to write, to type, and even to speak. At this time, the education of people with disabilities was very controversial. Most people thought that it was not possible or worthwhile to educate disabled people, but Helen and Anne proved how ridiculous this idea was. Helen attended regular schools and devoured literature, math, history, and foreign languages. Against all the odds, twenty-year-old Helen was accepted into prestigious Radcliffe College in 1900. Anne attended classes with her, signing the lectures into her hand. Four years later, Helen graduated at the very top of her class.

Helen devoted the rest of her life to writing and advocating the rights of the blind. Her first book, *The Story of My Life*, was published in 1903 and became a bestseller that has been translated into more than fifty languages. Soon afterward, Helen and Anne embarked on a lecturing tour of the United States and Europe. Helen spoke out for women's rights and international peace. Her most important work, however, was with the American Foundation for the Blind. Helen called for better education and employment for blind people, and through her celebrity she made the public aware of the changes that were necessary. For her courageous work, she was awarded the Presidential Medal of Freedom in 1964.

Helen attributed her success to her devoted teacher, Anne. In *The Story of My Life*, Helen wrote:

The most important day I remember in all my life is the one on which my teacher, Anne Mansfield Sullivan, came to me. I am filled with wonder when I consider the immeasurable contrasts between the two lives which it connects.... On the afternoon of that eventful day, I stood on the porch, dumb, expectant. I guessed vaguely from my mother's signs and from the hurrying to and fro in the house that something unusual was about to happen, so I went to the door and waited on the steps.... I felt approaching footsteps. I stretched out my hand as I supposed to my mother. Some one took it, and I was caught up and held close in the arms of her who had come to reveal all things to me, and, more than all things else, to love me.[12]

Helen and Anne had a close friendship and worked together until Anne's death in 1936. Together, they broke down barriers of education and discrimination, forever changing the way the world thinks of people with disabilities.

HOW WILL YOU ROCK THE WORLD?

I'm going to rock the world by opening a school that teaches teenagers how to care for children with special needs. My classes will increase teenagers' self-confidence and respect for all disabled people, while making it easier for parents of disabled children to find qualified sitters.

DEVORAH FRADKIN ✷ AGE 14

Anna Pavlova

1881–1931 ◈ BALLERINA ◈ RUSSIA

A gleam! a flash! a shimmering vision of beauty!
...Is it some creature from fairyland, some spirit
of ethereal grace freed from the terrestrial
trammels of the flesh? ... No. Merely Pavlova,
the incomparable Pavlova.

—*MANCHESTER EVENING NEWS*, 1925

The streets of St. Petersburg were covered in white snow. Everything glistened and shone under the streetlights as Anna's sleigh glided silently through the city. A snowflake landed on her nose, and she and her mother laughed with happiness. They were going to the ballet. Anna had never been, but just the word *ballet* seemed full of magic to her. "You are going to see the country of the fairies," her mother whispered. Anna couldn't wait.

The Mariinsky Theatre was the most beautiful place Anna had ever seen—the blue velvet, the gold paint, the lavish gowns, the gleaming chandeliers. As soon as she heard the music of Tchaikovsky and saw the ballerinas step into their dance of *Sleeping Beauty*, Anna began to tremble. It was all so beautiful, she was overwhelmed; she felt almost sick. Little Anna sat entranced until the lights came up again and she declared excitedly to her mother, "One day I will dance by myself, like Sleeping Beauty. One day I will, and in this very theater!" Her mother laughed, but Anna knew it was the truth.

Anna and the other students at the Imperial Ballet School often performed for the Tsar of Russia, Alexander III.

No one would have guessed that Anna would ever have the strength and stamina to become a dancer like she dreamed. She was born prematurely and was so small that her parents rushed to have her baptized so if she died, her soul would be saved. She surprised them and survived, but she was often ill. After her father died when Anna was two, she and her mother had very little money. Sometimes they had nothing to eat but rye bread and cabbage soup. Anna grew up undernourished and was a skinny, sickly child.

When Anna was eight, her mother saved every penny so she could give her daughter a special treat, the night at the ballet, the night Anna found her future. Her mother was skeptical of Anna's dreams but took her to the Imperial Ballet School to stop her pleading. When the school told Anna she was too young and would need to return and audition in two years, her mother thought that was the end of it. But not for Anna.

She spent the next two years imitating every move she saw that night at the ballet, and on her tenth birthday she went for her auditions. The examinations were difficult and competitive; about two hundred fifty children auditioned each year, and only twelve got in. But Anna's two years of hard work had paid off, and she was chosen. She immediately moved into the school. After a childhood of poverty, the Imperial Ballet School seemed like heaven on earth to Anna. Not only did she get three hearty meals a day, plus medical attention, she also studied dance, piano, acting, and pantomime.

After eight years of training, Anna graduated and joined the Imperial Ballet. At eighteen, she danced in her first public performance. Anna was unlike anything Russian audiences had ever seen. Tall, muscular dancers were the style of the time, while Anna was short and thin. But her unusual grace and fragile beauty set her apart, and her exquisite dancing caught everyone's attention. Within a few years she was promoted to prima ballerina (the ballet's star).

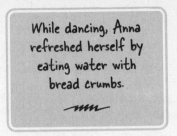

While dancing, Anna refreshed herself by eating water with bread crumbs.

As Anna's popularity grew, she left St. Petersburg and danced in the major cities of Russia. Before long, requests to see this new talent were pouring in from other countries as well, and soon, Anna was dancing all over Europe. Her fame spread across the Atlantic, and in 1910 Anna sailed to America, where she made her debut at New York City's world-famous Metropolitan Opera House.

Anna loved traveling and knew she could earn a great deal more money outside of Russia. So, although the Russian Ballet offered her the highest salary in its history, in 1912 she decided to leave her home country for good. She moved to a magnificent estate in London. A woman with many dreams, Anna now had the money to realize them. She started a dance school for young girls and also formed her own dance company.

With a family-like community of dancers to support, Anna and her troupe soon departed on a successful six-month tour of America. When they returned to Europe, political tension was high. Little did Anna know it would be the last time she would ever dance in Russia. The First World War was about to sweep across the continent and change life in Europe forever. Anna was performing in Berlin when the war started, but managed to get to England on one of the last boats to

Although Anna was small, her appetite was not. One interviewer wrote, "To see the delicate, fragile Pavlova, whose waist I could span with the fingers of my two hands, attack that two-inch steak made me gasp." She even drank gallons of cod liver oil in her efforts to put on weight!

When she was very busy dancing, Anna would use up to 2,000 pairs of ballet shoes a year! That's over five pairs each night!

cross the English Channel before war broke out! She took her company back to America, with no idea how they would support themselves while the world was at war.

Another of Anna's dreams was to expose all people, rich and poor, all over the world, to the beauty of ballet. So over the next decade she did her best to bring ballet to every corner of the globe, dancing in such exotic locations as Cuba, Costa Rica, Brazil, China, Japan, Indonesia, India, Egypt, and New Zealand. Anna introduced these countries to ballet, but they introduced her to their native dances and costumes. Because of her world travels, Anna's dances became more exotic and colorful.

Many of the countries she visited didn't have appropriate theaters to host the dancers. But that didn't stop Anna. In Mexico City, she and her company danced for thirty thousand fans inside a huge bullring! The heat was so intense that many of the dancers nearly passed out. Not Anna. Even when a tropical storm hit, she continued dancing in the rain until the stage became dangerously slick and they had to pull her off! The delighted crowd showered Anna with their sombreros.

Dancing is my gift and my life . . . God gave me this gift to bring delight to others. . . . I am haunted by the need to dance. . . . It is the purest expression of every emotion, earthly and spiritual. It is happiness.
—ANNA PAVLOVA

Throughout her career, but especially after the horrors of World War I, Anna was extremely compassionate and generous with her talents. She often gave benefit performances to raise money for wounded soldiers, war veterans, widows, orphans, the poor, and the homeless. She even adopted and raised a group of refugee girls. But her contributions never felt like enough to Anna, who said, "I can offer nothing but my art. It is a poor thing when such brave deeds are being done."

This desire to always do more drove her. In an interview she said, "I feel that, if I were ever quite satisfied, any power I possess would leave me. It is the divine discontent that drives us artists always onward." Although she had plenty of money to stop working, Anna never considered it. Even when she turned fifty years old, she would not retire. Her dedication may have hastened her death. In 1931, in between sold-out tours, Anna died from an illness made critical by her lack of rest.

In a time before airplanes and freeways, Anna traveled more than five hundred thousand miles, giving thousands of performances for millions of people. For most of these audiences, Anna was their first glimpse at ballet. And just as Anna the child began dreaming during her first visit to the ballet, Anna the prima ballerina spent the rest of her life introducing people to her dream, hoping to inspire the world.

HOW WILL YOU ROCK THE WORLD?

I want to be a contortionist! I want to get together a group of hypermobile people—who have really loose joints so are more flexible than average, like I am—and put on a show. After the show we would donate every cent to charity.

PAGE KIOSCHOS ☼ AGE 13

Coco Chanel

1883–1971 ◉ FASHION DESIGNER ◉ FRANCE

[Coco is] the woman with
the most sense in Europe.

—PABLO PICASSO, ARTIST

Gabrielle descended the staircase very, very carefully. Her ruffled purple velvet dress was long and heavy, and she was afraid she might trip. She couldn't wait to get to the graduation ceremony and see the looks on the faces of all her wealthy classmates. They wouldn't believe the lavish dress she had on—and they'd never guess she had designed and made it herself. But it was the look on her aunt's face that caught her attention.

"What, my dear, are you *wearing*? That dress looks horrible on you! Purple is not your color at all, and I can hardly see you under all those folds and feathers."

Gabrielle burst into tears and ran from the house as best she could in her awkward heels. She hated her cruel aunt, but Gabrielle knew in

Coco got her name
from a popular song
she sang as a chanteuse,
"Qui qu'a vu Coco?"
("Who Has Seen Coco?")
about a lost dog!

her heart that her aunt was right. She never looked good or felt at ease in the extravagant dresses that were the style. She loved simple, comfortable clothes. What *was* she doing in this hideous dress? She couldn't wait for the night to end.

Gabrielle would later become famous as Coco Chanel and would make her simple style the very symbol of understated wealth and elegance. She would enter the elite world she always yearned to be a part of; she would influence what the rich and famous wore. But she would never discuss her childhood.

Few of her upper-class friends and clients knew that the queen of fashion grew up as a peasant girl, in Auvergne, France. Her family was poor, and her mother died of tuberculosis when Gabrielle was a child. Her father, a traveling peddler, abandoned twelve-year-old Gabrielle and her two sisters at an orphanage, and they never saw him again.

Gabrielle's world was shattered, but she was too proud to show it. To the nuns at the orphanage, she was intelligent, a hard worker. As a teen she had to choose between becoming a nun and continuing school; she chose school. But it wasn't easy. At the convent boarding school, wealthy students were kept separate from the charity cases like Gabrielle. She was humiliated by the distinction and decided to earn money for herself and her sisters by working as a seamstress.

For her school graduation, she worked night and day at a nearby aunt's house to design an original dress. Influenced by the romance novels she read and the fashion of the day, Gabrielle created the gaudy, layered gown of purple velvet that prompted

Coco was not usually
the jealous type when
it came to her career,
but one over-the-top
designer so annoyed
her that when they
were introduced at a
ball, Coco asked her to
dance and then led her
so close to a candelabra
that her outrageous
gown caught on fire!

106

her aunt's sharp comment. Never again would she stray from her own innate sense of style. Simple clothes in subtle colors would become her calling card.

After her graduation, she worked by day as a seamstress and by night as a *chanteuse*, or singer. It was in the Paris cabarets that she received her nickname, Coco. Although she didn't have the best voice, Coco's personality couldn't be ignored; she was one of the most popular singers in Paris. Soon wealthy, influential men were courting her and introducing her to Europe's high society.

Although she wanted to fit in with the counts and countesses, the dukes and duchesses, Coco was always a little different. The buxom women around her dressed in heavy layers of ruffles and fabrics and cinched their bodies tightly with girdles and corsets. Coco said of their outrageous hats, which weighed almost as much as they did, "How can the brain function in those things?"

Coco, a flat-chested tomboy who loved riding horses, knew she couldn't compete with these fashion butterflies, so she showed off her slim figure and beautiful neck with simple outfits she made herself, even borrowing pants, shirts, and ties from her boyfriends. Her clothes were seen as radical, but her hats at least, were a hit. Instead of huge concoctions of fruit, flowers, and feathers, Coco designed smaller hats with a single feather, blossom, or even no adornment at all.

When she was twenty-five, Arthur Capel—a wealthy boyfriend—loaned Coco the money to start her own store and design studio in a posh Paris neighborhood. At first her look was criticized as "severe." But with the First World War underway, even the wealthy women were working for the war effort. Out went the ornate dresses and hats, the elaborate underclothes. They were considered extravagant when men were suffering. In came simpler clothes: the jersey suit, the safari coat, and the little

> Coco created the cardigan sweater when, on a cold day, she borrowed a boyfriend's pullover. To keep from messing up her hair while putting it on, Coco cut it down the front and added a ribbon along the rough edge. Every woman who saw her that day had to have one. They're still worn today.

> Unlike most designers, Coco never used sketches or patterns to create her clothes. She just draped fabric on a live model, took out scissors and pins, and cut, pushed, and pulled the cloth until another Chanel outfit emerged.

black dress. Coco designed outfits for a freer woman. Practicality was the rule; a woman had to be able to move easily in her clothes. Soon wealthy women of Paris and Europe demanded all her latest creations. Even the critics changed their tune and pronounced her clothes "elegant."

Coco's fashions echoed her childhood: simple cuts, like her old school uniforms, and neutral colors, especially black, like the nuns' habits. These plain outfits were accented with ornate jewelry, like a church with its stained glass windows. She was also inspired by the clothes of the poor: a sailor's pants and cap, a schoolgirl's simple dress. Although they reflected her humble origins, Coco's clothes weren't cheap. After her years of poverty, she made sure her rich clients paid her well, and she knew that a high price tag would only make her more in demand. As the 1920s approached, Coco set the standard for the "new woman:" slim; boyish; with bobbed, carefree hair; and financially independent. By the time she turned thirty, she was at the top of the fashion world.

She was also at the top of the social world. Always torn between creativity and financial security, wealthy Coco surrounded herself with artists. Pablo Picasso, Igor Stravinsky, Salvador Dalí—each counted Coco as a friend.

With her designs in high demand, Coco soon paid back her debt to Arthur Capel. But he married another woman soon afterward, since Coco's lower-class background made her unsuitable for marriage in his eyes. Coco was devastated, but she continued to see him even after the marriage. Their relationship ended when Arthur died in a car crash. For the rest of her life, Coco dated many men but never married.

By the time she turned fifty, in 1933, Coco's fashion empire employed nearly four thousand workers and sold close to twenty-eight designs each year! She also expanded into other areas of fashion. Her line of costume jewelry, which echoed the stained glass and church icons of her youth, was hugely successful. And when she set out to create a perfume, she knew it would have to be totally unique. Chanel No. 5 combined eighty flower essences, resulting in a fresh, youthful scent that lasted longer than other perfumes. Coco even made the bottle revolutionary; instead of the romantic, curvy bottles most perfumes came in, Coco created a strong, square, androgynous bottle with only her name and a mysterious number. People were intrigued. Soon Chanel No. 5 was the most popular perfume in the world.

The very nature of fashion is that what's in today is out tomorrow. But Coco was never out for long. Her style is so timeless that she was the height of fashion at the turn of the century and in the 1930s, then again in the 1950s. Even in the 1980s, after her death, Coco's style rose from the grave. Today, her look is still the epitome of elegant, understated style.

A poor orphan, with no class or connections, Coco made herself into a millionaire and founded the very first fashion empire. She created the movement toward functional, comfortable, and practical clothing for women, which has been copied by the likes of Calvin Klein, Ralph Lauren, and Tommy Hilfiger. Coco was the original. She freed women from the weight of fashion, allowing them to look beautiful and stylish in clothing that let them lead an active lifestyle. Coco's clothes were adored by women as varied as Princess Grace, Marilyn Monroe, and Jackie Kennedy, and her timeless style has defined women's fashion for almost a century.

ROCK ON!

JAZMIN WHITLEY

At age seventeen, Jazmin was the youngest clothing designer to ever launch at Los Angeles Fashion Week, and the next year she became the youngest designer to *show* at L.A. Fashion Week. She now has six clothing lines. She influences pop culture through her designs and her television show, *House of Jazmin*.

Bessie Smith

1894–1937 ◦ SINGER ◦ UNITED STATES

*Bessie used to thrill me at all times. It's the way she
could phrase a note in her blues, a certain something
in her voice that no other singer could get....she had ...
music in her soul and felt everything she did.*

—LOUIS ARMSTRONG, JAZZ TRUMPET PLAYER

Little Bessie's throat was getting tired. She'd been singing out-side the market all day long. Lots of people passed by, and many stopped to listen to the sweet voice of the nine-year-old girl dressed in her Sunday best. But not too many left money in her hat. Her stom-ach was growling for dinner, and she couldn't wait to get home. But as she looked down at the few coins sitting in her hat, she knew it wasn't enough. With no mother or father to support them, her brothers and sisters were counting on her. She would just have to stay a little longer. A small crowd gathered as Bessie belted out a soulful tune that gave them all goose bumps. She had no idea that soon she'd be singing on a

As an African American, Bessie often faced segregation and prejudice when she toured, but she refused to be intimidated. One day, when she was threatened by members of the Ku Klux Klan, Bessie scared them away, yelling, "You better pick up them sheets and run!"

~~~

real stage. Bessie was about to be discovered. In time, this frail young girl would become known as the Empress of the Blues.

Elizabeth Smith was born on April 15, 1894, in Chattanooga, Tennessee, a bustling town of about thirty thousand people. About 40 percent of Chattanooga's population was made up of African Americans, many of whom struggled to make ends meet. In a time of racial discrimination and segregation, African American families had to work hard just to scrape by. Since both of Bessie's parents died at a young age, she and her siblings earned money any way they could. Throughout her childhood Bessie spent her days singing on the streets for pocket change.

When Bessie was nine years old, she made her stage debut in a local theater. She earned eight dollars for her performance. In 1912, Bessie's oldest brother was working for a traveling show, and when they returned to Chattanooga he convinced the managers to audition his talented sister. They hired her as a dancer because they already had a singer in Gertrude "Ma" Rainey. Ma Rainey was impressed with Bessie's voice and later recruited her for the Rabbit Foot Minstrels, a famous African-American performance troupe.

Soon Bessie's music became so popular that she could perform on her own. She traveled throughout the South, playing in theaters, clubs, and meeting halls. In 1921 Bessie started performing in northern cities too. Her raw, powerful voice drew large crowds, and she became well-known for her dramatic style.

Bessie made her first record, "Down Hearted Blues," in 1923, and by the end of the year, it had sold over 750,000 copies. In the course of her career, she made more than 150 recordings and sold up to ten million records. This is an amazing total, since Bessie sang at a time when many people didn't even own record players! She was often accompanied by the most talented musicians of the day, including trumpeter Louis Armstrong, pianist Fletcher Henderson, and trombonist Charlie Green.

In 1937 Bessie died from injuries sustained in a car accident. She was only forty-three, but she lived a full, hard life in her short years. This unparalleled singer experienced firsthand the highs and lows that were the subjects of her music. She triumphed over poverty and prejudice. She went from being a poor street singer to the celebrated Empress of the Blues. Today, Bessie's many blues recordings are still considered some of the best of all time.

> "The greatest blues singer in the world will never stop singing" are the words carved on Bessie's tombstone, which was purchased by Janis Joplin and other donors in 1970. Before that, Bessie's grave had been unmarked.

HOW WILL YOU ROCK THE WORLD?

My dream is to become a singer because when I sing I feel like I'm in another world. I will follow in the footsteps of my two mentors: my dad and the great Kelly Clarkson!

KELSEY MIDDLETON AGE 10

Irène Joliot-Curie

1897–1956 ◦ CHEMIST ◦ FRANCE

A task once begun develops in an unexpected fashion, opening new paths for future work. And thus we satisfy our spirit of adventure.

—IRÈNE JOLIOT-CURIE

Irène was surrounded by army doctors, medical equipment, and wounded soldiers. Blood was everywhere, and she could hear the battle raging in the distance over the cries of the sick and dying men around her. But eighteen-year-old Irène Curie was used to these horrifying distractions and focused her attention on setting up the new machine. The French doctors and nurses at the army hospital wondered what young Irène's mysterious contraption was all about.

When she finished setting up, Irène asked for a patient to volunteer. The doctors and nurses gasped in amazement as the soldier's leg bone magically appeared on the screen before them. They could see completely *inside* his leg—through the skin, the blood, and the muscle—right to the bone. And they could see exactly where the bone was broken.

> Irène was very athletic and loved the outdoors. Her favorite sports were biking, skiing, swimming, and mountain climbing, all of which she continued throughout her life.
>
> ~~~

Irène was showing them the radioactive technology she and her mother had been working on: the groundbreaking X-ray machine!

Irène Curie was born to Nobel Prize–winning scientists Pierre and Marie Curie on September 12, 1897, in Paris. Her parents spent much of their time working, so she and her younger sister were largely raised by their grandfather, especially after Pierre's death in 1906. Irène was a quiet and thoughtful child who loved nature, poetry, and reading, but most of all, science. Although many girls were discouraged from studying math and science at the time, Marie Curie strongly supported her daughters' education in these subjects.

In fact, Marie considered most French schools too narrow in their academic offerings, so she started a cooperative school for her daughters and eight other children of university professors. The professors themselves taught lessons in art, literature, science, math, English, and German. The cooperative school lasted only a couple of years, though, and after that Irène spent two years at a private girls' school. She later attended the prestigious Sorbonne University in Paris and received her doctoral degree for her study of alpha particles in 1925.

Throughout her life, Irène was greatly inspired by her mother. Marie Curie was the first woman to earn a doctoral degree in France, the first woman to teach at Sorbonne, and the first woman in the world to win a Nobel Prize (she won two: the first in physics and the second in chemistry). Irène learned a lot from her mother, and they often worked together.

When World War I broke out, Irène and Marie put together X-ray units for the battlefront. Irène traveled to the French front lines to set them up and teach people how to use them. She showed doctors and nurses how to take X-rays of soldiers' wounds and how to locate bone breaks and pieces of shrapnel in the images. She then helped surgeons determine the best angle from which to enter the wounds for treatment.

After the war, Irène continued as her mother's assistant at the Radium Institute of the University of Paris. There she met her future husband and research partner, Frédéric Joliot. They married in 1926 and had two children: Hélène in 1927 and Pierre in 1932.

After their marriage, Irène and Frédéric began referring to themselves as the Joliot-Curies. Together, they conducted groundbreaking experiments and wrote hundreds of reports. In 1934 Irène and Frédéric began experimenting with two metals, polonium and aluminum. Their results led them to a revolutionary discovery: they could create artificial radioactivity! This discovery earned Irène and Frédéric the 1935 Nobel Prize in chemistry. With this award, Irène and her mother, Marie, became the only mother and daughter to both win a Nobel Prize.

Sadly, Marie couldn't share in her daughter's triumph. At the time, no one knew how deadly it was to be exposed to radioactive chemicals. Because of her intense contact with these chemicals in her research, Marie died of leukemia one year before Irène's Nobel Prize was awarded.

After her mother's death, Irène continued her research, and Frédéric started work as a scientist at the Collège de France. Irène became a strong supporter for women's rights and was a member of the National Committee of the Union of French Women. In 1936 she became one of the first female cabinet members in France when she was named as the undersecretary of state for scientific research. She was also a member of the World Peace Council and an officer of the French Legion of Honor.

Irène remained committed to her research, and in 1938 she conducted another groundbreaking experiment. Although she considered her conclusions useless because they did not support what she was working on, later scientists repeated her experiment and realized that Irène had actually discovered nuclear fission (the splitting apart of atoms). Her results were analyzed by nuclear physicists and laid the crucial foundation for this important area of study.

Irène dedicated her life to her research and continued working in the

> Irène and Frédéric had two children. Hélène would grow up to be a physicist and Pierre a biologist.
>
> ∼∼∼

laboratory until her death in 1956. Like her mother, she also died of leukemia, giving her life for her work. The French government organized a national funeral to honor the life of this great scientist who made some of the most significant scientific discoveries of her time.

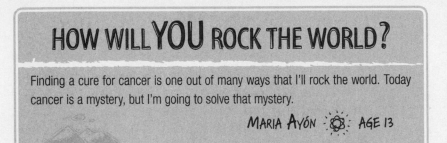

HOW WILL YOU ROCK THE WORLD?

Finding a cure for cancer is one out of many ways that I'll rock the world. Today cancer is a mystery, but I'm going to solve that mystery.

MARIA AYÓN ☀ AGE 13

Marian Anderson

1897–1993 ◈ SINGER ◈ UNITED STATES

*A voice like yours is heard
only once in a hundred years.*

—ARTURO TOSCANINI, CONDUCTOR, COMPLIMENTING MARIAN

Voice coach Giuseppe Boghetti barely looked up when the teenage girl walked in. He frowned and continued scribbling notes onto his sheet music.

"You know," he barked, "I'm seeing you just as a favor to your principal."

Marian could feel her body trembling. Could she really bring herself to sing for this man? Mr. Boghetti was one of the most well-respected voice coaches in the country. Why should he listen to her?

"I don't want any new students. I have too many already." Her heart sank more, but he waved his hand at her to begin singing.

To calm her nerves, she closed her eyes and tried to forget where she was and who she was singing for. As she sang her favorite spiritual,

Marian never had problems projecting her voice. As a girl, her mother told her to imagine the black people who were only given seats way in the balconies. She always made sure those back seats could hear her voice too.

"Deep River," Marian's rich, powerful voice poured out over the room, "Deep river, my home is over Jordan...."

She finished and opened her eyes. The room was silent. Mr. Boghetti had his eyes closed too, and seemed to be frozen, holding his breath. *Oh no, he hated it!* Marian thought in a panic.

After an eternity, the gruff teacher opened his eyes and looked at Marian for a long time. "I will make room for you right away," he said.

She clamped her hands over her mouth so she wouldn't scream from happiness.

"I will need only two years with you. After that you will be able to go anywhere and sing for anybody."

Marian was overjoyed—but now she had a different worry. She wondered if the money her church had raised for her music lessons would be enough. Mr. Boghetti's fees would not be cheap. But when she asked him about it, he surprised her again. He said he would waive his regular fees; he would teach Marian for free. She couldn't believe her luck! Finally, her dreams were coming true. Maybe she really would be a famous concert singer.

Marian was born in 1897 in Philadelphia, Pennsylvania. Her father worked hard delivering ice and coal, and he made enough money so her mother could stay home and take care of the children. Marian grew up in a happy family, surrounded by lots of love. From a very early age, she loved music, but her parents couldn't afford to buy instruments or lessons. So Marian made her own music. At age three she began to sing.

By the time she was six, she was the star of her church choir. Her voice was deep and rich; she was what musicians call a contralto, the lowest female voice, but she could sing higher notes and lower notes as well. In fact, when her choir learned a song, Marian taught herself *all* the parts, high and low, so if a singer missed a performance, Marian could fill in for her.

Her family's life became much more difficult when Marian turned twelve and her father died in a work accident. Her mother had to clean people's houses to support the family, and though she never complained, she worked nonstop to keep her children fed and clothed. Marian desperately wanted to help. Although she dreamed of being a singer, she began training for more practical work; she learned to type so she could become a secretary and help support the family when she finished high school.

Her voice, however, was so amazing that throughout high school people hired her to sing at church gatherings, parties, and club meetings, paying her five dollars for each performance. This was a lot of money to Marian; she began to think that maybe she wouldn't have to become a secretary after all. But she knew that to be a professional singer, she would need professional training.

She decided to apply for lessons at a local music school, but they turned her away with a harsh rejection: "We don't take colored." Marian was crushed. She knew racism existed, but she had grown up in a neighborhood where whites and blacks respected each other. This was the first time Marian experienced racism *personally*, and she was horrified. She was ready to give up her singing dreams right then and there. "The way that woman spoke, it bit into my soul," she told her mother. "You must have faith," was the answer her mother gave back. "There will be another way for you to learn what you need to know."

And there was another way. Marian's church believed in her dreams, so when the members heard about her troubles, they raised money for private lessons. That's how she came to audition for Giuseppe Boghetti. That year she graduated from high school and began to sing professionally all over Pennsylvania at churches, colleges, and small theaters. Her fee went up to one hundred dollars per show! It was the happiest day in Marian's life when she told her mother, "I can take care of you now. You don't have to work anymore."

When Marian first sailed to Europe, she was the only black person on board. For the entire two-week voyage, Marian had to stay alone, separate from the rest of the white passengers.

Even when Marian came to Washington to sing at the Lincoln Memorial, she wasn't allowed into any hotels and had to stay in a private home.

—um—

In 1925 Marian got her big break. She entered a singing contest with three hundred competitors; first prize was a concert in New York City with the New York Philharmonic Orchestra. Marian surprised many, including herself, when she won. Her performance with the famous orchestra was a success, and Marian had every reason to believe her career was underway and that invitations to sing in America's best concert halls would pour in.

She was mistaken. Although the Civil War had freed the slaves almost sixty years before, America was still a very segregated and racist place. Jim Crow laws (named for an obedient black character in a minstrel show) barred blacks from sitting in the same seats as whites on buses or trains, from eating in the same restaurants, and even from performing on the same stages. Signs all over America read "Whites Only." Marian wasn't invited to sing in America's best concert halls because she was black, and even when she could sing in those halls, many white ticket buyers didn't believe a black woman could have any talent.

With her career in America at a standstill, Marian decided her only option was Europe. She left in 1930 and toured there for the next five years. Although she was still unknown in America, she was accepted as a great singer in Europe and even sang for the kings and queens of Sweden, Norway, Denmark, and England. Marian was very happy abroad, not just with her success, but because the weight of racism was lifted from her shoulders: she could sit in any seat, stay at any hotel, eat at any restaurant, perform anywhere she wanted, and earn a living as a singer. Europeans didn't care about her skin color, just her voice. But she missed her family and home. She dreamed of returning to America and making it a better place to live and perform.

One night at a Paris concert hall, Marian was performing, and sitting in the audience was Sol Hurok, manager of some of the world's greatest stars (he helped launch Anna Pavlova's career, among others). After the show, he asked Marian if he could represent her on her return to America. It was another dream come true. Fellow show biz experts warned Hurok that America still wasn't ready. "You won't be able to give her away," they predicted. Not much had changed in five years.

But with Sol's help, Marian made a triumphant return to America in 1935 with a concert in New York's famous Town Hall. The audience gave her a standing ovation, and the critics raved, "Marian Anderson has returned to her native land one of the great singers of our time." She was home.

In 1939, after singing in most European capitals, Marian tried to arrange a concert in Washington, DC. The theater, Constitution Hall, was owned by the Daughters of the American Revolution (DAR), a group of women whose families had, years ago, fought for America's freedom from England. Ironically, these women, descendants of men who fought for freedom, refused to let Marian sing on their stage. It was for "white artists only." First Lady Eleanor Roosevelt, herself a DAR member, resigned from the group in protest. The event sparked one of the first great civil rights debates of the twentieth century: Americans of both colors argued openly about the rights of blacks and waited to see what would happen.

What happened was a quiet revolution. Marian was invited instead to sing a free concert in front of the Lincoln Memorial. It was a symbolic location for the event, at the foot of a statue of the man who drafted the Emancipation Proclamation, freeing the slaves. The concert drew an unbelievable seventy-five thousand fans (and millions more on radio). Marian was so astonished by the show of support that afterward she remembered nothing of her time on stage. The audience, however, would never forget it.

She opened with "America," and one observer recalled blacks and whites in the audience singing along with

> Orpheus Fisher first asked Marian to marry him just after high school. She said no because she knew it would interfere with her career. Over the next 20 years, while Marian worked on achieving her dreams, Fisher waited for her. Marian finally said yes, and they married in 1943.

Marian, "My country, 'tis of thee, sweet land of li-ber-ty, of thee I sing." He said later, "She put such great emphasis upon 'liberty.' The DAR's refusal to allow her to sing was a breach of that liberty.... There were tears in my eyes. I think there were tears in the eyes of almost everybody in that huge crowd."[13] When she finished with " ...let freedom ring," America was listening. One journalist applauded Marian's courage: "That concert...struck at the very depths of racism in America." Years before Martin Luther King Jr. would stand in the same spot and deliver his "I Have a Dream" speech, Marian Anderson pricked the nation's conscience with her own dreams of equality.

She continued breaking through the color barrier for the rest of her career. She performed at the White House and at presidential inaugurations; she sang in Russia, Israel, and Japan; and during World War II, she finally appeared at Constitution Hall. In 1955 she achieved yet another of her goals: she became the first black person to perform at the world-famous Metropolitan Opera in New York City. Again, the audience members showed their support for Marian's efforts in changing America. They gave her a standing ovation even *before* she began singing her part.

Her every childhood dream realized, Marian kept on singing. In 1957 the State Department sent her on a twelve-nation tour as a goodwill ambassador for America. A year later they made her position official and appointed Marian as a delegate to the United Nations. Marian didn't retire from singing until she was almost seventy years old, giving a farewell tour of the United States in 1964–65. During her career, she was honored with countless awards, including the 1939 Spingarn Medal, given to the black American who achieved the most, and the 1963 Presidential Medal of Freedom, the highest award a president can give a citizen during peacetime.

Many people believe that because of Marian's pure voice and tremendous range, she was the world's greatest contralto. But her impact was not limited to her voice. Her obituary summed up Marian's lasting memory: "[She] maintained a quiet dignity while transcending the racial and cultural barriers imposed on her artistry." She showed Americans—black and white—what blacks could do if given the chance. Her success opened music to all the black artists who followed her—Stevie Wonder,

Diana Ross, Michael Jackson, and even Mariah Carey—and made it one of the first fields in which black Americans could achieve greatness and be recognized for their talents. Her courage and insistence on the right of every American to pursue her dreams also paved the way for future civil rights heroes like Rosa Parks and Martin Luther King Jr. and the great racial change of the mid-twentieth century.

ROCK ON!

CHARICE PEMPENGCO

When Charice was four years old, her mother noticed that her daughter had a strong voice. With some vocal lessons and practice, Charice was soon competing in talent shows like *Little Big Star* in the Philippines and *Star King* in South Korea. When a fan posted her competition videos on YouTube, an international following instantly sprang up. The young Filipina now has six albums and was featured on *The Oprah Show*.

Golda Meir

1898–1978 ✦ PRIME MINISTER ✦ ISRAEL

*There is only one thing I hope to see before I die,
and that is that my people should not need expressions
of sympathy anymore.*

—GOLDA MEIR

N o daughter of mine is going to stand on a box in the street and make a spectacle of herself. It is a *shandeh* (disgrace)!" shouted Golda's father, his face red with fury. Seventeen-year-old Golda tried to explain that she had already promised herself and her friends that she would give the speech in front of the synagogue. She tried to explain that her past speeches had been very successful at getting the neighborhood Jews excited about helping their comrades in far-off Palestine. But her angry father didn't hear a word she said as he yelled, "If you go, I will follow you and pull you home by your braid!" Golda went anyway, but she could feel her body shaking as she climbed atop her box to speak to the large crowd.

Because she worked mornings in the shop, Golda was often late for school. A policeman lectured Golda's mother about truancy, but since she spoke little English, she didn't understand him. Golda continued being late.

She spoke passionately about the brave Jews in Palestine, men *and* women, who were struggling to create a nation where all Jews around the world would be welcome and safe from persecution. Thankfully, she couldn't see her father in the crowd, but she could see the eyes of her audience lighting up with pride and determination. At the end of her speech, the crowd responded with a long roar of applause, and even more people volunteered to help the cause. Golda wondered if maybe her father hadn't come after all. When she returned home to face her father's punishment, her mother met her at the door. "Your father is asleep now," she said, "but he did hear you speak. He was amazed. He said to me, 'I don't know where she gets it from.'" Golda's father was so moved by her words that he forgot his threat entirely. Golda considered it the most successful speech she ever made.

Golda Mabovitch, born in 1898, spent the first five years of her life in Kiev, Russia. Even at such a young age, Golda experienced the struggles of the Jewish people of Europe. Mobs of angry Russians often destroyed the homes and shops of their Jewish neighbors, sometimes even beating and killing them. But Russian police did nothing to help the Jews. When the Jewish community protested the brutality by holding a one-day fast, five-year-old Golda insisted on fasting too, against her family's wishes.

It didn't take long for Golda's father to realize that it was getting too dangerous to be Jewish and live in Russia. He decided to move his family to the United States. After a long and dangerous journey, eight-year-old Golda and her family arrived in America and settled in Milwaukee, Wisconsin. At first Golda was overwhelmed by all the extravagances of America—running water, electric lights, trolleys, flushing toilets—but soon she happily settled into the large community of Russian Jews in her neighborhood. Her mother set up a general store below their apartment, and Golda opened it in the mornings while her mother bought supplies at the market.

Golda loved school and was a good student. At age eleven, she began the public speaking and fund-raising that would make her so famous later in life. When she realized that many of her classmates couldn't afford to buy their own schoolbooks, Golda recruited a group of girls to raise money. They called themselves the American Young Sisters Society and organized a ball, which attracted dozens of people. They served food and read poetry, and Golda gave a speech. The event was so successful that they raised enough money to buy books for all the poor children of the school.

During Golda's childhood, most people didn't go to high school, especially not girls—most went to work or got married as teens. When Golda told her parents that she planned to go to high school and then to college, they began secret negotiations to marry her off to a man twice her age! Golda found out and ran away to live with her older sister in Denver, Colorado.

In Denver she not only went to high school but also got involved in the growing Zionist movement. The Zionists believed that the Jewish people should create a new nation in their ancient homeland. Thousands of years ago, the Jewish religion was founded in the deserts of the Middle East (which they called Zion), where they lived peacefully until the Romans drove them out and renamed the area Palestine. The Jews spread out around the world, mostly in countries that didn't want them, and many longed to return. Golda was inspired by what she heard of the Jewish pioneers in Palestine who were working to reclaim the desert and create a Jewish nation. To support their efforts, Golda spent hours on the streets of Denver raising money for Jewish pioneers to buy

> At 71, Golda returned to her Milwaukee grade school, which by then was mostly populated by African American students instead of Jewish. The students greeted her with the Israeli anthem, "Hatikvah," and a white rose made of tissue. She carried the rose back to Israel with her.

During Hitler's reign, successful Jewish doctors, teachers, lawyers, and businessmen fled to Palestine to start over as farmers and laborers.

~~~

Palestinian land from the Turkish and Arab landowners.

Golda returned home, entered a teacher's college, and became even more active in the Zionist movement. Although she was too young, members of the Labor Zionist Party were so impressed with Golda's work, they accepted her into the party at age seventeen. In 1917 nineteen-year-old Golda decided it was time to go to Palestine herself to help build the Jewish nation she'd been dreaming of all her life. Before she left, she married Morris Meyerson, a man she'd fallen in love with back in Denver. They left for Palestine together in 1921.

Golda and Morris moved onto a *kibbutz* (a community of people living and working together toward common goals). The group raised and grew all their own food, built communal housing, and shared everything—money, clothes, even children! Kibbutzes across Palestine were working to transform desert into productive farms so that Jews could have a place to live that would sustain them. Golda loved the work and was good at making improvements. She was soon elected to make decisions for her kibbutz and to help decide the future of other Jewish settlements in Palestine. Golda had never been happier.

She and her husband took a break from the kibbutz to start a family, and Golda gave birth to a son and then a daughter. Although she loved her children, Golda missed her work. After four years of domestic life, Golda decided to return to creating a nation for the Jews. She was a passionate, hard worker, and she soon became a leader of the growing nation.

In the 1930s, just as Golda's political life began taking off, life for Jews in Europe was deteriorating rapidly. All over Europe, they were being persecuted more strongly than before, and in Germany, Hitler and his Nazis began attacking the Jews. Seventy thousand refugees fled to Palestine, their only safe haven. The Arabs of Palestine, however, strongly opposed increased Jewish immigration. They attacked

Jewish settlements and demanded the British government (the colonial power in the area) stop letting refugees in. In 1939, just as Hitler was forcing European Jews into his deadly concentration camps, the British put the brakes on immigration and outlawed

From 1945 to 1950, half a million Jewish refugees flooded Palestine!

the purchase of Arab land. The Zionists were enraged. They knew their European family and friends would die if they couldn't get to Palestine. They felt they had no choice but to fight.

Golda joined Haganah, the Jewish secret underground army, which began smuggling as many Jewish refugees as possible into Palestine. Boats were built in secret and sent to rescue European Jews. Upon returning, the boats had to sneak past the British blockade of ships and unload the refugees in the dark of night. Back on shore, also under a cloak of darkness, members of the Haganah would carry pre-built housing to a new village site. When the sun came up, there would be a new town full of rescued immigrants! Golda's increased workload and worry over saving European Jews put a strain on her marriage, and in 1941 she and her husband separated.

In 1946, after World War II ended, England decided to let the Jews create their nation, but Golda and her government knew that when the British pulled out, surrounding Arab countries would move in and attack. Golda went to the United States to raise money for weapons to protect the future nation. In a fund-raising speech in Chicago, Golda proudly said to the Jewish crowd, "You cannot decide whether we will fight or not. We will....Whether we live or not, this is a decision you have to make." Her speeches were so effective that she returned with fifty million dollars for the army. Her fellow politicians were

Golda endangered her own life by trying to build peace with the opposition. She disguised herself as an Arab woman and traveled through enemy territory to meet with the leader of a neighboring Arab country. Sadly, her courageous bid for peace was unsuccessful.

In Moscow, Golda was greeted by over 50,000 Russian Jews, who came to meet her and celebrate the founding of Israel. They were defying their oppressive government, and their courage affected Golda deeply.

astounded at the fortune Golda raised and credited her with saving the country from certain doom.

In 1948 the United Nations took a vote, and the Jewish nation of Israel was born. Israel's leaders were elated and signed a proclamation of independence, outlining the goals of their new nation. As Golda signed her name, she wept uncontrollably. When someone asked why she was crying, Golda replied, "Because it breaks my heart to think of all those who should have been here today and are not."

Fights between the Jews and the Arabs began almost immediately. Thanks to Golda's fund-raising, Israel was able to defend itself from all attacks. In a rush of national pride, Golda changed her name from Meyerson to the Hebrew Meir and began work in the new government, first as Israel's ambassador to Russia, then as minister of labor. When she became foreign minister, Israel responded to threats from Egypt by capturing their territory—the Sinai Peninsula and the Gaza Strip. Explaining Israel's attack to the United Nations, Golda said, "We desire nothing more than peace, but we cannot equate peace merely with an apathetic readiness to be destroyed." And again in 1967, when the countries around Israel joined together in a plan to "push the Jews into the sea," the Jews launched a surprise attack and won a complete victory.

After forty years of hard work establishing a country for the Jews, Golda was ready to retire. Israel, however, wasn't ready to let her go. When the prime minister died in 1969, Golda was asked to replace him. At age seventy-one, Golda became the leader of the Jewish nation she had dreamed of as a teen. During her five years as prime minister, Golda exhausted herself building the country up and defending it from enemy countries and terrorists. Even after resigning from her post, she continued to work for peace, meeting with Egypt's president Anwar Sadat in 1977.

In 1978 Golda's strength finally gave out, and she died of the cancer she had been secretly battling for fifteen years. To the people of Israel, Golda will always be a symbol of their nation's birth, and she will be remembered for guiding the country through its most challenging and exciting period in history. The rest of us will remain in awe of her progression from a young girl fund-raising for her poorer classmates to the prime minister of Israel.

HOW WILL YOU ROCK THE WORLD?

If I could rock the world, I would stop the terrorists and make them see sense. They would then see that all of their fighting is irrational, and they would destroy all of their weapons. They would not enforce hate and violence, but enforce love and peace all over the Middle East in places like Libya, Iraq, and Afghanistan.

SARAH BIGLEY ⚛ AGE 14

Queen Sālote Tupou III

1900–1965 ◦ QUEEN ◦ TONGA

Beyond her wisdom and abilities there was always her strong affection for her people, young and old. Her love for them was heartily reciprocated. Now, many years after her death, the Tongans still speak of her as "Our Beloved Queen."

—DR. A. H. WOOD

Royal families from all over the world came to attend the coronation of Queen Elizabeth II, but Queen Sālote Tupou III was startlingly different from the rest. This strong, passionate leader wore a traditional Tongan *ta'ovala* (a ceremonial matting worn around the waist) along with her European-style clothing. Rain poured down on London the day of the coronation ceremony, but Queen Sālote insisted on riding in an open carriage. She waved to the huge crowds lining the streets, and they cheered enthusiastically.

By the end of the journey, Queen Sālote was soaked! When the astonished royalty asked why she had not allowed the carriage's hood to

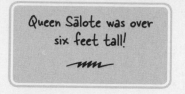

Queen Sālote was over six feet tall!

be raised, she smiled and charmingly explained that she thought it only fair to endure the rain just like the British citizens who had watched the procession through the downpour. She also told them that she was following an ancient Tongan tradition that one could not cover oneself when a higher-ranked ruler—in this case, the queen of England—was present. Queen Sālote's preservation of tradition and her love for the people characterized her entire reign as ruler of Tonga.

Sālote Mafile'o Pilolevu was born into the ruling family of Tonga, an island nation in the southwest Pacific Ocean, on March 13, 1900. When she was nine, she traveled to New Zealand to be educated. She returned to Tonga and got married when she was seventeen.

Sālote's father died the next year, and she became queen of Tonga at the age of eighteen. She was officially crowned Sālote Tupou III on October 11, 1918. At the coronation, she wore a ta'ovala that was handed down from her ancestors. The six-hundred-year-old ta'ovala was a symbol of the ancient gods.

At the time, Tonga was a British protectorate: an independent kingdom protected and influenced by England. During Queen Sālote's rule, England's power over Tonga was decreased. However, Tonga's ties to England were still strong, and Queen Sālote was often honored by the British government. In return, Tonga provided troops and support for England during World War II.

Queen Sālote was greatly loved by her people because she worked hard to improve the country. She promoted agricultural development, health reform, and better living conditions as well as education for all Tongan people. She was especially interested in improving the welfare of women. The queen promoted education for girls, and she was active in the Pan-Pacific and South-East Asia Women's Association.

Queen Sālote loved the ancient traditions of her country, and she advocated the preservation of Tongan culture. She formed and presided over an organization that encouraged the creation of traditional Tongan crafts for personal use and for sale to tourists. The queen formed the Tonga Traditions Committee in 1954.

Queen Sālote believed in having a strong connection with her people. She sent gifts to people in need, and her palace was open to everyone. Queen Sālote celebrated Tongan culture through poetry and song. She wrote poems about history, tradition, nature, and everyday Tongan life. The poems were then set to music that she composed.

Dr. A. H. Wood, a friend of Queen Sālote, wrote this about her:

In a procession three kilometres long 10,000 children were allowed to enter the Palace grounds and wave to the Queen as she sat on the verandah. Obviously in poor health, she nevertheless . . . received their greetings with undisguised delight. It was the last occasion on which the Tongan people saw their Queen.[14]

December 16, 1965, was a sad day for the Tongan people. Early in the morning, their beloved Queen Sālote died. A ruler for forty-seven years, Queen Sālote enjoyed the longest reign in Tonga's history and will forever be remembered as a wise, gracious, and caring queen.

ROCK ON!

ROSICLÉIA DA SILVA

Growing up in the Amazon region of Brazil, Rosicléia da Silva has witnessed deforestation's toll on the environment firsthand. When she was still in grade school, she helped start Agenda 21, a program to help the environment on the local, national, and global levels. Since then, she's also been involved with Millennium Developmental Goal 7, which strives to ensure environmental sustainability by 2015. She has also represented Brazil at the J8 Summit and has been featured on UNICEF Radio—all while still in her teens!

FRida Kahlo

1907–1954 ❀ PAINTER ❀ MEXICO

*The only thing I know is that I paint
because I need to.*

—FRIDA KAHLO

Frida rested in a bed at the Red Cross Hospital. The pain in her body was agonizing—her spine was broken in three places, and her pelvis, right leg, and foot were shattered. It was a miracle that the eighteen-year-old girl was alive at all. The doctors hadn't expected her to survive after a streetcar smashed into the bus she was riding. But she did survive, only to be wracked with unbearable pain, night and day. As her body healed in the hospital, Frida thought she would lose her mind. She could barely sleep, but being awake was even worse—hours and hours with nothing but the pain!

After several months, in desperation, she had a nurse bring art supplies to her bed. As Frida concentrated on putting paint on the canvas, her mind no longer focused on the misery of her body. Her brush became an outlet for the physical and emotional pain she was enduring. Still in her teens, Frida had found her life's work, a career that would bring her fame and respect throughout the world.

Frida Kahlo was born near Mexico City on July 6, 1907. She was one of five children of a German-Jewish photographer and a Mexican woman of Indian and Spanish descent. When she was fifteen, Frida was accepted into Mexico's prestigious National Preparatory School as one of thirty-five girls out of two thousand students. Frida was a bright girl; she studied literature and art, and she hoped to one day become a doctor.

When she was eighteen years old, Frida's life was changed forever. She was in a horrible traffic accident, and overnight she went from a young, healthy, carefree girl to a girl who would struggle for the rest of her life with physical disabilities and pain. Fortunately, Frida found an outlet for her powerful emotions—painting.

Although she had no formal art training, Frida's work was strikingly mature. Her paintings, most of which were self-portraits, expressed her personal experiences and her complex feelings. In 1929 she married Diego Rivera, Mexico's most famous painter, whom she had met years before her accident while he was painting a mural at her school. Theirs was a passionate but stormy relationship. Frida's paintings captured her conflicted feelings for Diego and the pain of being childless. (She couldn't have children because of her injuries.) Frida's unique style drew upon popular Mexican art as well as surrealism. Using bright colors and powerful, symbolic images, Frida bared her soul to the world.

> Frida had an endless curiosity about the world around her. She was known to cram all sorts of things into her school bag, including drawings, butterflies, dried flowers, and illustrated books from her father's library.

During the 1940s, Frida began showing her work internationally. Her raw, bold style was quite unusual and shocked most people who saw it. Despite this, her work won great critical acclaim. In 1953 she held her first major solo exhibition in Mexico. It was a huge success. Although she was very ill at the time of her first exhibition, Frida insisted on being carried to the opening on her bed.

Several months later, Frida's health problems worsened, and one of her legs had to be amputated. But she found a way to make the best of the situation. Instead of being embarrassed and trying to hide her disability, she wore a red velvet boot with bells on her artificial leg.

Frida's health problems continued until her death in 1954. After she died, her home was made into the Frida Kahlo Museum. It holds not only Frida's original paintings but also her extensive collection of Mexican folk art. In 1985 the Mexican government declared Frida's paintings to be national treasures. The beautiful and vivid intensity of her art has earned her a place on the list of the greatest artists in Mexico's history.

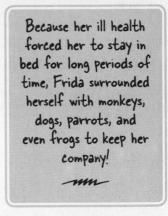

Because her ill health forced her to stay in bed for long periods of time, Frida surrounded herself with monkeys, dogs, parrots, and even frogs to keep her company!

André Breton, a poet and art critic, indicates how the beauty of Frida's art often disguises its power: "The art of Frida Kahlo is a ribbon around a bomb."[15] And Diego Rivera, Frida's husband, observes of her work, "Frida is the unique example in the history of art of someone who tore open the breast and heart in order to speak the biological truth of what is felt within them."[16]

HOW WILL YOU ROCK THE WORLD?

I will rock the world by becoming a great and famous painter. I will paint inspiring pictures with joyful colors to decorate the walls of hospitals, schools, and nursing homes. My paintings will soothe and calm people, creating atmospheres that help learning, healing, and relaxing. The world will smile with my art.

ALTA BROCHA MISHVLOVIN ⚙ AGE 14

MotheR TeResa

1910–1997 ⊗ MISSIONARY ⊗ MACEDONIA AND INDIA

The poor do not need our compassion or our pity;
they need our help. What they give to us is more
than what we give to them.

—MOTHER TERESA

Young Agnes knelt in front of the cross. The church was empty, and she was alone. She felt at peace as she gazed up at the statue of Jesus. She often thought about how he dedicated his life to serving the poor and loving the people others called unlovables—the prostitutes, the handicapped, and all the others who were outcast. For his work and his message of equality and forgiveness, he was killed. As she knelt before him, Agnes felt a strong conviction that stayed with her for the rest of her life. She too would help the poor and love the unlovables. From that day forward, twelve-year-old Agnes knew that she would be a nun. This young girl's simple desire to help the unfortunate would eventually blossom into a global fight against poverty.

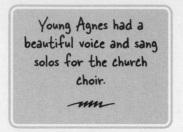

Young Agnes had a beautiful voice and sang solos for the church choir.

Agnes Gonxha Bojaxhiu was born on August 26, 1910, in Skopje, Macedonia. She was the youngest of three children born to an Albanian couple. Agnes's father died when she was still a young child, and her mother began making dresses to support the family. Agnes's mother also did charity work, and she took her daughter along on visits to the elderly, the sick, and the poor. A quiet and thoughtful child, Agnes enjoyed helping people in need. She was also deeply religious and often went alone to her Catholic church to pray.

By the age of twelve, Agnes had received her life's calling. She joined the Loreto nuns and traveled to Darjeeling, India, when she was only eighteen. After she took her first official vows as a nun and chose her new name, Sister Teresa (the patron saint of missionaries), she was sent to Calcutta to teach at St. Mary's, a school located in a convent and run by the nuns. Sister Teresa's work as a humanitarian had begun.

Sister Teresa worked at St. Mary's for twenty years, eventually becoming the headmistress. But she became increasingly disturbed by the horrible conditions of the people outside the convent walls. Calcutta's streets were crowded with homeless children, beggars, and lepers, many of them sick and starving. These were the people that Jesus had loved and preached about.

On September 10, 1946, Sister Teresa was on a train going to Darjeeling when she received what she described as another call from God. This "call within my calling" told her that she was to leave the convent and the school and to help the poor while living among them. She could not disobey. She left the convent and went out into the streets of Calcutta.

On the first day of her new "school," only five students joined Sister Teresa. She used a stick to scrape lessons in the dirt.

Sister Teresa had a special love for children, so she immediately focused on helping the young people in the slums. She began by starting

144

an informal school for them. In addition to basic language and math skills, Sister Teresa taught the children how to keep themselves clean in order to avoid certain diseases.

In 1950 Sister Teresa started her own order of nuns devoted to helping the poor. They were called the Missionaries of Charity. As the order's leader, she became Mother Teresa. The work was hard and the days were long, but young nuns poured in from around the world to join the new order. The nuns of the Missionaries of Charity woke up at 4:30 AM to attend a worship service and eat breakfast. Then they went out into the city slums, where they worked until lunchtime. After lunch, they said their prayers and took a short rest. Then it was back to work until after dark.

The Missionaries of Charity continued to grow, largely due to the leadership and enthusiasm of Mother Teresa. In 1952 she opened Nirmal Hriday ("Pure Heart"), a home for the dying. Fatally ill patients were brought to the residence so they could die with peace and dignity. Mother Teresa then founded the first of her many orphanages, and she opened clinics for lepers and other people with severe disabilities. Over the years, Mother Teresa's work spread around the entire world.

During Mother Teresa's lifetime, the Missionaries of Charity opened facilities in five continents and 95 countries.

Mother Teresa's devotion to her cause brought her many awards and honors, which she accepted not for herself but on behalf of the poor and poverty-stricken throughout the world. Her awards included the Nobel Peace Prize, India's Padma Shri award, the US Presidential Medal of Freedom, the Pope John XXIII Peace Prize, Great Britain's Templeton Prize for Progress in Religion, the Philippines' Ramon Magsaysay Award for Peace and International Understanding, and the Jewel of India Award.

The last few years of Mother Teresa's life were marked by lung, kidney, and heart problems, but she continued her missionary work. In 1997 she died at the age of eighty-seven, but the Missionaries of Charity are still working toward her humanitarian vision. Mother Teresa was respected and loved by rich and poor, young and old, in every corner of the globe. Millions of people mourned the passing of this visionary who had a special love for helping children: a modest woman who started her charitable work while still only a child herself.

HOW WILL YOU ROCK THE WORLD?

I plan to rock the world by helping people and by bringing different cultures together. I have spent ten years living overseas. This taught me that there are lots of people all over the world who are different and who need help. We all have differences, but in the end we are all equal. If people understand that, they can help each other and create peace. If people understand that, we can live in a different world.

MOLLY MASTRORILLI ☼ AGE 13

MaRy Leakey

1913–1996 ❀ ARCHAEOLOGIST AND ANTHROPOLOGIST
ENGLAND AND AFRICA

For me it was the sheer instinctive joy of collecting, or indeed one
could say treasure hunting: it seemed that this whole area abounded
in objects of beauty and great intrinsic interest that could be
taken from the ground.

—MARY LEAKEY

Mary kneeled down over the ground, patiently and meticulously scanning the surface for fossils. Suddenly, something caught her attention. To most, it would look like just a dirty rock, but to Mary's trained eyes, it was a piece of human history. Bulging out from the ground was a fossilized bit of bone. Mary carefully brushed away the dirt around it to reveal two teeth and a curving jaw. Eventually, she would unearth more than four hundred pieces of the ancient skull. After the fragments were fitted together, analysis showed that the skull belonged to a pre-human ancestor who lived 1.75 million years ago.

Mary's find proved that humanlike creatures existed much earlier than most scientists previously believed. This revolutionary discovery was just one of many important contributions Mary made to the study of archaeology.

Mary Nicol was born on February 6, 1913, in London, England. Her father was a landscape painter with a true passion for archaeology. He shared this love with Mary when she was still a young girl, taking her with him on expeditions to France, Italy, and Switzerland. Mary learned how to excavate and use other techniques by assisting archaeologists as they uncovered and deciphered Stone Age cave paintings in France.

Mary didn't go to school like other children, but she learned how to read and draw from her father. Mary was only thirteen years old when her father died. At first her mother tried sending her to convent schools, but Mary wasn't used to learning in a traditional school environment. After Mary was expelled from two institutions, her mother gave up.

Meanwhile, Mary was learning in her own way by attending lectures at museums and universities. When she was just seventeen, Mary assisted at an archaeological site in southern England, directed by archaeologist Dorothy Liddell. Dorothy showed Mary that women could be successful in archaeology, a traditionally male-dominated field. Encouraged, Mary began sketching high-quality pictures of the tools at the site.

One day another archaeologist, Gertrude Caton-Thompson, saw young Mary's drawings. She was very impressed and asked Mary to draw some ancient tools that had been discovered in Egypt. Gertrude introduced Mary to Louis Leakey, an anthropologist who worked in Africa. Louis was writing a book on his work and asked Mary to illustrate it. Mary joined him in Africa and began working on the illustrations and on the dig site. Working side by side and sharing their mutual passion for archaeology, it wasn't long before Mary and Louis fell in love. In 1936 they married.

One of Mary's favorite activities was watching the wildebeest migrate in the Serengeti, and even after she was not working there anymore, she returned once a year for the migration.

Over the next few years, Mary and Louis worked in various sites in Africa. Among Mary's finds were a cremation ground, ancient tools, and pottery. She made her first famous discovery in 1948, when she dug up the eighteen-million-year-old skull of a pre-human ancestor.

In 1959 Mary made perhaps the greatest find of her career: the skull of a human predecessor that was 1.75 million years old. Before Mary's discovery, scientists believed that humanlike creatures had existed for only several hundred thousand years. Mary's discovery proved them all wrong!

> Mary didn't like to theorize about how the fossils she discovered fit into the timeline of human evolution. "What I came to do was to dig things up and take them out as well as I could," she said.[17]

Soon after that, she discovered a set of ancient humanlike footprints that were 3.7 million years old. This indicated that early human ancestors walked upright much earlier than scientists had previously thought.

Mary continued to live in Africa until her death in 1996. Her groundbreaking work opened the door for girls of the future who wanted to grow up to be archaeologists, scientists, and adventurers. Through Mary's archaeological explorations and expertise, theories about the history of human development were changed forever. She remarked, "What I have done in my life I have done because I wanted to do it and because it interested me. I just happen to be a woman, and I don't believe it has made much difference."[18]

ROCK ON!

REFILWE TSUMANE

Young historian and political activist Refilwe Tsumane believes it's important to recognize society's "unsung heroes." She was one of the winners of the 2008 Albert Luthuli Young Historians Oral History Competition for her recognition of South Africa's grave diggers. She also represented South Africa at the 2009 J8 Summit, in which young ambassadors from around the world offer recommendations on global issues to G8 world leaders.

Jackie Mitchell

APPROXIMATELY 1914–1987 ◈ ATHLETE ◈ UNITED STATES

I had a drop pitch and when
I was throwing it right,
you couldn't touch it.

—JACKIE MITCHELL

Jackie scuffed the pitcher's mound with her cleats and glanced up at the batter standing beside home plate. Babe Ruth tipped his cap to her.

Can I do it? thought Jackie. *Can I strike out the Home Run King? The Sultan of Swat? The number one home run hitter in the major leagues?*

The crowds in the stands were laughing, as if this match-up between baseball's biggest hero and an unknown seventeen-year-old rookie—a girl, of all things—was the funniest thing they'd ever seen. Jackie heard a few jeers, but she didn't let them rattle her. She rubbed the ball between her fingers and thought about all the years she'd been practicing. Jackie had been playing baseball for as long as she could remember. She thought about all the people she'd struck out with her left-handed pitch—plenty of them men.

Babe was smirking now, as if to say, "C'mon little girl, let's see what you've got."

I'll show you what I've got, thought Jackie, rocking back for her windup. The ball sailed forward. Babe swung at it, but it dipped just before reaching the plate. A sinker.

"Steee-rike one!"

Babe had missed. His eyes popped open in surprise. Jackie could almost hear the crowd's disbelief. *A strike? Thrown by a girl?* Babe gripped the bat tighter. He wasn't smirking anymore.

Before the big game, Babe Ruth told reporters: "I don't know what's going to happen if they begin to let women in baseball. Of course, they will never make good. Why? Because they are too delicate. It would kill them to play ball every day."

Jackie's next two pitches were balls. After the second one, the crowd laughed again, figuring the first strike was just a fluke. Babe laughed along with them. But Jackie didn't let it rattle her. For her fourth pitch, she threw another sinker. Babe swung at it and...

"Steee-rike two!"

Now Babe was mad. He glared at Jackie. She knew he'd expect another sinker, so instead she threw the ball straight over the plate. Babe didn't swing this time, convinced it was another ball.

"Steee-rike three!"

The crowd went wild. Four thousand people were clapping and yelling and chanting, "Jackie! Jackie!" She'd done it! Jackie Mitchell had struck out the superstar of baseball. Babe kicked at the plate, called the umpire a few choice names, then threw his bat down in disgust, and stomped back to the dugout. Jackie just smiled, enjoying her moment in the sun.

It seems Virne Beatrice "Jackie" Mitchell was always destined to be the underdog. When she was born around 1914, she weighed just three and a half pounds. But her size and sex didn't hold her back. As soon as Jackie could walk, her father took her to the ballpark and began teaching her to play baseball. Even as a toddler, little Jackie was good at it, really good.

The Mitchell family lived next door to a minor-league baseball player named Dazzy Vance (a future Hall of Fame pitcher for the Brooklyn Dodgers). Dazzy took an interest in young Jackie. He could see her passion for the game and her talent on the field. When Jackie was around five years old, Dazzy taught her his favorite pitch, the sinker, a curveball that drops just before home plate. It's a tough pitch to hit and a tough pitch to throw, but Jackie mastered it quickly. By age seven she was a star in the sandlots of her hometown, Memphis.

Although the press at the time heralded Jackie as the first-ever woman to play in the minor leagues, that's inaccurate. In 1898 Lizzie Arlington played one game for a minor league team in Reading, Pennsylvania.

When Jackie was growing up, women had been playing baseball for decades. But they didn't play on men's teams. Bloomer Girls, all-female teams, barnstormed across America playing against local, semi-pro, and minor-league men's teams. These female players did well against the men, often beating them, but there were no women on any minor or major league baseball teams. Jackie hoped to change that.

At age sixteen, she played on a women's team in Chattanooga, Tennessee, and a year later she was invited to an elite baseball camp in Atlanta run by former major league pitcher Kid Elberfeld. Jackie was the only girl at the camp. Like Dazzy, Kid saw Jackie's potential and helped with her training. Soon word got out: Jackie could pitch. Joe Engel, a former pro pitcher, heard about the girl wonder and came scouting. He offered her a contract to play on the minor-league

After the famous game against the Yankees, Jackie got tons of fan mail. Some of it was simply addressed to "The Girl Who Struck Out Babe Ruth."

team he owned: the Chattanooga Lookouts. Jackie was thrilled, and when she signed the contract she became the second woman in history to join a minor league baseball team.

Just a few days after signing the contract, Jackie's new team was scheduled to play an exhibition game against the major league New York Yankees. It was the off-season, and these exhibition games were a common way for major league players to stay in shape and for smaller towns to get a chance to watch their heroes play. No one expected much from the Lookouts.

The manager didn't choose Jackie as their starting pitcher, however. Jackie watched from the dugout as their first pitcher gave up a double and then a single, putting the Yankees ahead 1–0. Third up to bat was Babe Ruth. The undisputed superstar of baseball in the 1920s and '30s, Babe held the record for hits and home runs.

The manager waved Jackie to the mound. It was her turn to pitch. To everyone's surprise, in five pitches Jackie struck out the Sultan of Swat. Some fans thought it must be a publicity stunt, but if so, Babe was one heck of an actor. He cursed the umpire and threw a fit before leaving the field.

> After being cut from the Lookouts, Jackie barnstormed with the House of David, a team famous for their long hair and beards. Jackie sometimes wore a fake beard during their games.

Next up was Lou Gehrig, the Iron Horse, major league's second strongest batter after Babe. *Could she do it again, or was Babe a one-time fluke?* the crowd wondered. Jackie pitched three times, Lou swung three times, and he missed three times. She'd done it again: Jackie had struck out the strongest duo in baseball. The four thousand fans in the stands rose to their feet and gave Jackie a standing ovation that lasted several minutes.

After such a stunning debut, Jackie expected a long career in baseball. But that wasn't to be. The game against the Yankees attracted attention around the world. There were photos in dozens of newspapers and magazines, and a newsreel of Jackie's strikeouts played in theaters across the country. Just a few days after the game, the baseball commissioner canceled Jackie's contract with the Lookouts. He declared women unfit to play baseball because the game was "too strenuous" for them. More likely, he didn't want any more girls embarrassing his male stars.

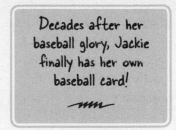

Decades after her baseball glory, Jackie finally has her own baseball card!

Despite her voided contract, Jackie managed to pitch in the minor leagues for a few more years, playing for small, unknown teams and keeping her name out of the headlines. But she missed pitching to the best of the best, and she knew her dreams of pitching in the World Series would never be. Jackie retired from baseball in 1937 at age twenty-three. Major League Baseball formally banned women from playing in 1952, and as of 2012 there are still no women players.

In 1982, more than fifty years after her historic game, Jackie was invited to throw the Opening Day first pitch for the Chattanooga Lookouts. She died five years later. What kind of mark would Jackie have made if not for pro baseball's sexism? Would she have pitched in the World Series? Would her name be as recognized as Babe Ruth's? We'll never know. But we do know that Jackie's story has inspired generations of female athletes. There are girls today playing against boys in Little League and dreaming of pitching like "The Girl Who Struck Out Babe Ruth."

HOW WILL YOU ROCK THE WORLD?

I will rock the world by opening a museum about girls' sports. Most people don't think girls can do some sports. But girls can do anything that they want. I think the museum will inspire girls to rock the world in anything they do.

SAMANTHA DANIELS · AGE 13

Babe Didrikson Zaharias

1911–1956 ✸ ATHLETE ✸ UNITED STATES

You are looking at the most flawless section of muscle harmony, of complete mental and physical coordination the world of sport has ever known.

—GRANTLAND RICE, SPORTSWRITER

It was Babe's first basketball game playing for the Golden Cyclones, a semiprofessional team. They were playing the national champions, the Sun Oil team, and her teammates were nervous. But Babe wasn't nervous. She ran and passed and shot the ball, again and again and again. By the end, the Golden Cyclones had won the game, and Babe had scored more baskets than the entire Sun Oil team combined! The other girls were amazed by the super-athlete, but they had no idea that Babe would become one of the greatest athletes of all time. She excelled at almost every sport she tried, including golf, track, baseball, archery, skeet shooting, swimming, diving, horseback riding, and billiards, to name just a few. Her life set an inspiring example for all

There were several rows of hedges in Babe's neighborhood, which she loved jumping over during her runs. Later she would earn an Olympic gold medal in the hurdles.

—〰〰—

female athletes who followed in her footsteps.

Mildred Ella Didrikson was born on June 26, 1911, in Port Arthur, Texas. Her family was very poor, and she and her six brothers and sisters all had to help out. Mildred picked figs and sewed potato sacks for money. Sports were her way of having fun. Early on she decided that she would be the greatest athlete ever.

As a young girl, she was such a powerful home-run hitter that kids nicknamed her "Babe" after the famous slugger, Babe Ruth. Her father built a gym in the backyard, and out of all her brothers and sisters, Babe used it the most. She worked out on the gym's chin-up bars and weightlifting equipment. She also played baseball and basketball with the kids in the neighborhood.

In high school, Babe went out for every sport open to girls. She earned a spot on the basketball team and soon became a star. Her athletic ability attracted the attention of Melvin McCombs, the manager of a company-sponsored women's basketball team. He recruited Babe to play on his team, the Golden Cyclones, and she led them to a national championship. In 1930 she was selected All-American Forward.

Babe decided to try track and field next. In 1932 she competed in the Amateur Athletic Union women's national championship. Out of eight events, Babe won five, tied for first in another, and took second in another. Babe earned enough points to win the team title all by herself!

Her outstanding track victories at the national championship led Babe to the 1932 Olympics in Los Angeles. As she left for the games, she told reporters that she planned "to beat everybody in sight." And beat them she did. Babe won a gold medal and set the world record in the javelin throw, won another gold medal in the hurdles, and won a silver medal in the high jump!

While she was in Los Angeles, Babe played her first round of golf. Her natural ability was impressive. A few years later, Babe decided to make a career out of the sport. She practiced hard, sometimes for fifteen or sixteen hours a day, and her hard work paid off when she won the Texas Women's Invitational golf tournament in 1935. She remembered:

Weekends I put in twelve and sixteen hours a day on golf....I'd drill and drill and drill on the different kinds of shots. I'd hit balls until my hands were bloody and sore....After it got too late to practice any more, I went home and had my dinner. Then I'd go to bed with the golf rule book.[19]

In 1938 Babe met wrestler George Zaharias at a golf tournament, and the two were married in less than a year. Babe continued her golf career, winning an incredible seventeen tournaments in a row! She was the first American to win the Ladies' British Amateur Championship. But Babe's biggest impact on women's golf was yet to come. In 1949 she helped to found the Ladies Professional Golf Association. This organization sponsored professional women's golf tournaments, which attracted more and more women to the sport. Today, LPGA tournaments offer millions of dollars in prize money for professional woman golfers.

Babe wrote this in her autobiography:

Before I was even into my teens, I knew exactly what I wanted to be when I grew up. My goal was to be the greatest athlete that ever lived. I suppose I was born with the urge to get into sports, and the ability to do pretty well at it....Now there's nobody who wants to win more than I do. I'll knock myself out to do it. But I've never played rough or dirty. To me good sportsmanship is just as important as winning....You have to play the game the right way. If you win through bad sportsmanship, that's no real victory in my book.[20]

In 1953 Babe was diagnosed with cancer. She fought the disease with her usual determination, and after undergoing surgery, Babe recovered and

> When Babe returned to Texas after the Olympics, she rode into her hometown in the fire chief's car at the head of a parade held in her honor. They gave her the key to the city.

159

miraculously won the US Women's Open Golf Tournament in 1954. Babe persevered like a champion for two more years, but in 1956 the cancer returned. The world's greatest female athlete died at the age of forty-two.

Throughout her life, Babe earned prestigious awards and honors. She was the only woman to be named the Associated Press's Female Athlete of the Year six times! She was also voted the Woman Athlete of the Half Century in 1950 and was inducted into the World Golf Hall of Fame in 1951. Sports historians ranked her as the second most outstanding and influential athlete in American sports history, just after Babe Ruth. Babe Didrikson's legacy has passed on to today's female athletes. Her talent and determination opened doors for women to compete and succeed in the world of sports.

HOW WILL YOU ROCK THE WORLD?

I will rock the world by making horseback riding a well-known Olympic sport, like ice skating or gymnastics. The sport of horseback riding doesn't receive the attention it deserves, and until it does, I'll keep spreading the horse-world word!

BRIANNA YORK ☼ AGE 13

Indira Gandhi

1917–1984 ✳ PRIME MINISTER ✳ INDIA

*I cannot understand how anyone can be an Indian and
not be proud—the richness and infinite variety of our composite
heritage, the magnificence of the people's spirit, equal to any
disaster or burden, firm in their faith, gay spontaneously even
in poverty and hardship.*

—INDIRA GANDHI

Twelve-year-old Indira sat nervously with her schoolbooks in the backseat of a car. She had just left a secret meeting where the top leaders of India's National Congress Party were planning the next step in their rebellion against the British. At that time, India was a British colony, and India's people were struggling to gain their independence.

As Indira's car reached the tall iron gates, a police inspector ordered her driver to stop. Indira's heart raced. If the police searched the car, she

> Indira's earliest memory was of her family burning clothes and other items made outside India in a nonviolent boycott of European goods. Little Indira threw her own European—made doll in the flames.
>
> ～

would be caught and put in jail along with many leaders of the rebellion. The brave girl hid her fear by impatiently demanding that the inspector let her pass; she was late for school and had no time for these delays. The police believed her and let her go. Little did they know that hidden safely in her trunk were all the secret documents of the independence movement!

As her car passed through the gate, Indira looked out the back window and saw that the police had already surrounded the house. Inside, the leaders watched nervously as Indira's car escaped. Fearing a raid on their headquarters, the Indian leaders had placed all their most important papers in the trunk of the young girl's car. It was vital that the British not get their hands on those documents, and thanks to Indira, they were safe. This daring act of bravery was just the beginning of Indira's career of devotion to her country: the twelve-year-old girl would go on to become the first woman leader of a democracy and one of the most powerful and influential politicians in the world.

Indira Priyadarshini Nehru was born on November 19, 1917, in Allahabad, India. Her country had been ruled by England for over 160 years. The British invaders controlled everything, and Indian citizens had little to no power in their own country. Any Indians who spoke out in favor of Indian independence were thrown in jail. As the only child of Jawaharlal and Kamala Nehru, leaders in India's struggle for independence, Indira spent a lot of her childhood without her parents. Her mother and father were often in jail. But their work inspired Indira, who, even as a child, loved India with a passion and did all she could to help the revolutionary National Congress Party.

When Indira was twelve, she helped organize more than one thousand Indian children into a group called the Monkey Brigade. They helped the Congress Party in everyday tasks like addressing envelopes, writing announcements, and cooking food. More importantly, Indira's group spied on the British police. While they pretended to play, the children would eavesdrop on police conversations, listening for news of any upcoming arrests. Then they reported back to the Congress Party. By giving activists time to hide, the Monkey Brigade's early warnings often prevented arrests. The police never suspected that these innocent-looking kids were actually spies!

In 1937 Indira was accepted into Oxford University in England. While studying in England, Indira got engaged to a childhood friend, Feroze Gandhi, and the two were married in 1942 after they returned to India.

Upon her arrival back in India, Indira found her beloved country in the midst of the bloodiest fighting of the entire rebellion. She immediately dove back into her work in the party, and it wasn't long before the British learned of her rebellious activities. Indira was thrown in prison for eight months! But she didn't lose hope. She and the other activists were making great progress. In 1947 the British gave up the fight. After almost two hundred years of colonialism, India finally won its independence!

As the most popular leader in the National Congress Party, Indira's father became the first prime minister of India after the war. Indira's mother had died in 1936, so Indira acted as her father's first lady, adviser, and ambassador to other countries. She was still active in many political organizations, and in 1959 she was elected president of the National Congress Party. This was a post both her father and grandfather had held; it made her the second-highest-ranking politician in India.

When Indira's father died in 1964, Lal Shastri became prime minister, and he appointed Indira as minister of information and broadcasting. In a country where few people could read, radio and television held great power for bringing news and information to *all* the people of India, not just the rich and educated. Indira made great

> England was fighting World War II while Indira studied there. She drove an ambulance to help with the British war effort. But at the same time back in India, the British had put her father in jail again.

163

> Indira's hero was Joan
> of Arc, who also fought
> for her country's
> independence from
> invaders.
> ᨆᨆ

progress by doubling the number of radio and television programs and producing inexpensive radios. She was also the first person to open up the airwaves to *anyone* who wished to speak; even critics of the government were free to voice their ideas. India was becoming a true democracy.

Two years later, Shastri died, and Indira was elected prime minister of India. She was the first woman ever to run a democratic country—and the world's most populated and diverse democracy at that! Her newly independent country was plagued with problems and threats to its freedom. Many people didn't think she could handle the responsibility, and even some members of the National Congress Party initially thought she would be easy for them to manipulate. But Indira proved to be a powerful and skillful leader.

During her term, Indira strengthened India's international influence and kept both the United States and the Soviet Union from exerting their control over her nation. She led India to victory in a bloody war with Pakistan and sent the country's first satellite into space. At home she launched the Garibi Hatao (Remove Poverty) campaign to help limit population growth and improve the quality of life for India's poorer citizens. Indira was reelected in 1971, despite some growing opposition.

Throughout Indira's second term as prime minister, criticism of her policies mounted steadily. She had created voluntary sterilization—a procedure in which people who don't want to have more children can be made physically unable to do so—to help limit the population and curb poverty, but her enemies claimed it was forced. In 1975 riots and protests against her became so severe that Indira declared a state of emergency. She imprisoned political opponents and censored the press. Though these short-term undemocratic practices were no longer in effect by the 1977 election, Indira was voted out of office. She spent the next two years regaining support and was reelected by a landslide in 1979.

Indira continued her work to improve the country she loved, but she still faced strong opposition. In 1984 Indira ordered a controversial raid on a temple that was held by Sikh separatists. A few months later,

Indira was assassinated by two of her Sikh bodyguards in an act that many view as retaliation.

Indira's will was found after her assassination. She said:

If I die a violent death as some fear and a few are plotting, I know the violence will be in the thought and action of the assassin, not in my dying—for no hate is dark enough to overshadow the extent of my love for my people and my country.[21]

Though her time as a leader was full of controversy, Indira helped her nation through the transition from colonial rule to democracy. She ruled during a challenging and trouble-plagued time in India's history. Through it all, her love of her country and its people was clear, and her intentions to promote the welfare of India prevailed. A strong and confident woman, Indira left her mark as a powerful leader who aspired to advance one of the largest, poorest, and most diverse democracies in the world.

ROCK ON!

NEHA GUPTA

At the age of nine, Neha Gupta founded the nonprofit organization Empower Orphans. The goal of Empower Orphans is to create self-sufficiency among orphaned, abandoned, and underprivileged children by supplying them with the tools to gain a basic education and the technical skills needed to enable a sustainable livelihood. Empower Orphans has raised more than $250,000 in cash and has positively impacted the lives of more than 15,000 children. Neha has opened multiple libraries, computer labs, sewing centers, and science labs, and she has been honored with several awards including being selected as the Philadelphia 76ers Hometown Hero, the Great Friends to Kids Award, the Kohl's Care Scholarship, and the prestigious World of Children Award.

Eva "Evita" Perón

1919–1952 ⊙ ACTRESS AND POLITICIAN ⊙ ARGENTINA

I should rather say that the world at the moment suffers from a lack of women. Everything, absolutely everything in this world, has been conducted on men's terms.

—EVITA PERÓN, CELEBRATING ARGENTINE WOMEN WINNING THE RIGHT TO VOTE

As Eva and her brothers and sisters filed past the coffin, she could feel the angry eyes of the crowd behind her burning a hole in her back. She could hardly see her dead father through her stinging tears of grief and shame. When he was alive, her father had been married to another woman and had other children. Eva's mother was his mistress, and Eva and her siblings were his second, secret family. Second families were common among the rich men of Argentina, but they were objects of scorn to the upper class. In their small agricultural town, Eva and her family were outcasts.

Eva knew that her mother broke an unspoken rule by coming to the funeral. Her dead father's wealthy friends were appalled to have

167

During her time as a radio star, Eva began a radio program dramatizing the lives of famous women. A revolutionary idea in machismo Argentina!

━━━

these poor, sinful, lower-class people in their midst. In her shabby dress, Eva could feel their scorn. As the anger and shame swelled inside her, seven-year-old Eva promised herself that one day she would have their respect—one day *she* would be the one with the wealth and power.

After her lover's death, Eva's mother worried how she would take care of her family without his support. All the land and businesses were owned by a few wealthy families who refused to help out the poorer people in town. Eventually the family moved to the small town of Junín, Argentina, and into a tiny, cramped apartment above an Italian restaurant. Some people say Eva's mother opened a boarding house to support her family, but others say she became a prostitute. Eva's older sisters got jobs and went to school, but Eva wasn't interested. She was starstruck and dreamed of becoming an actress. It was an impossible dream for a poor girl from the country. But Eva was not an average girl.

In 1934 fifteen-year-old Eva left Junín for the big city—Buenos Aires—determined to be a star. Eva wasn't the only one leaving the country behind for city dreams. During the 1930s Buenos Aires was attracting droves of poor people from the countryside who couldn't find work. Competition for jobs was severe, and many people went hungry. For five long years, Eva struggled to earn a living by working bit parts in stage and radio shows. Finally, just as she turned twenty, she got her first big break with a large role on a radio drama series.

Over the next few years, Eva blossomed into a star. She was making good money, so she could afford to dress more elegantly. And in true starlet style, she dyed her brown hair blond. She also learned how to play the game of politics. When a military regime seized power in Argentina, Eva quickly became friends with several officers in the new government.

In 1944, at a fund-raiser, Eva met the man who would share her passions for the rest of her life. Although Colonel Juan Domingo Perón arrived with a throng of beautiful women, by the end of the evening, he had eyes only for Eva. Perón was a handsome forty-eight-year-old widower who was beginning to make a name for himself in politics, especially for his role in winning higher wages and benefits for lower-class workers. He was drawn to twenty-five-year-old Eva's beauty but also to her intelligence and ambition. But most importantly, Juan and Eva shared similar backgrounds—they were both children of forbidden relationships between a rich man and a woman of the lowest social class. Both knew how it felt to struggle against prejudices, and both had worked hard for their success. They shared a mutual respect.

Just a month after they met, Juan was promoted to vice president of a new government, and Eva began doing patriotic radio shows, promoting Juan and his ideas. These shows were hugely popular and helped make Perón a household name. Eva also became president of the actors' union and more active in Juan's political decisions. At twenty-six, the once-poor, lower-class girl from the country was already a millionaire.

Juan and Eva became so popular and so powerful that the government felt threatened by them. Juan was arrested, and Eva was fired from her radio job. But the arrest only increased the couple's popularity among the poor and working-class people of Argentina, who held a daylong strike and demonstration demanding Juan's release. It brought the capitol to a standstill. Juan was freed, and the lower classes felt they'd won their first battle against the rich who controlled government, land, jobs . . . everything. The Peróns seemed like their only hope. They gave Eva the affectionate nickname by which she would always be known—Evita.

Just after his release, Juan and Evita were married in a secret ceremony. Juan announced he would run for president, and Evita got her job back and continued promoting Juan

> When Evita became first lady, the wealthy women of Argentina snubbed her because of her lower-class roots. Evita got revenge by closing down their favorite charity and starting one of her own just like it. When the rich women protested, she had them thrown in jail for a few days!

169

over the radio. While most politicians were wealthy and relied on the rich, land-owning voters to get them into office, the Peróns focused on the poor and working-class voters and the trade unions for support. Juan and Evita, with their own humble backgrounds, came to represent the poor, who were proud of who they were for the first time in Argentine history. "I feel myself responsible for the humble," said Evita, "as though I *were* the mother of all of them."

In 1946 Juan was elected president by a large margin. At twenty-seven, Evita finally had the power she had always dreamed of. In a time when women had little power in their own homes, let alone a voice in government, Evita broke all the molds. She was determined to close the gap between the rich and the poor. She set up an office at the Ministry of Labour and forced companies to grant benefits and salary increases to workers in the trade unions. She also directed the Social Aid Foundation, raising fifty to one hundred million dollars a year to build hospitals, schools, and homes for the poor.

But Evita's greatest contribution was her fight for women's equality. At that time, women in Argentina could not vote. Evita organized rallies and gave regularly scheduled radio talks, passionately urging Congress and the people of Argentina to grant women an equal place in society. Her speeches were successful, and in 1947 Argentine women won the right to vote.

Evita also campaigned for legal rights and equal pay for women. At the time, women were paid only half as much as men doing the same jobs, so Evita helped form and run the Peronista Women's Party. In 1949 women working in the textile industry won equal pay, and a law was passed that increased women's wages in all other jobs to 80 percent of men's salaries. A law was also passed that gave women legal equality in marriage and custody of their children. Eva even went so far as to request that stay-at-home mothers and housewives be paid for their work!

If you want to learn more about Evita's life, check out the movie EVITA starring Madonna and Antonio Banderas.

In 1950 Eva shocked the country once again by announcing she would run for vice president. Eva's tri-

170

umphs, however, weren't enough to blot out the growing accusations of corruption and greed that people voiced against her, Juan, and their government. Their popularity was on the decline. Public opposition was so strong that Eva was forced to withdraw from the race, although her husband remained on the ballot.

> I want nothing for myself. My glory is and always will be . . . the banner of my people, and even if I leave shreds of my life on the wayside I know that you will gather them up in my name and carry them like a flag to victory.
> —EVITA PERÓN

The years of exhausting work—of rising at eight in the morning and working until midnight—finally began to take their toll on Eva's health. Just before voters went to the polls, Evita was diagnosed with cancer. The election instantly became charged with emotion. Over 90 percent of eligible women voted for the first time, and Juan Perón won by a landslide.

The tarnish on Evita's reputation was virtually wiped clean, as thousands of people held prayer vigils for her recovery. She was declared Spiritual Leader of the Nation and Evita Capitana (Captain Evita). Her autobiography became an instant bestseller and was required reading in schools and universities. Despite winning back the love of her people, Evita died on July 26, 1952.

During her thirty-three years, Evita was an inspiration to the poor and working-class people of Argentina and to the women of the world. Against amazing odds, she went from a poor, illegitimate, uneducated country girl to one of the most wealthy, powerful, and revolutionary women in the world. She gave people hope that even the most unfortunate person could rise to great heights. Evita fought for the rights of those people who had no voice, and she forced the government to hear them, thus becoming the symbol of their hopes and dreams. For people around the world who continue to struggle against many forms of oppression in their countries, Evita is a true legend who will never be forgotten.

HOW WILL YOU ROCK THE WORLD?

I want to rock the world by helping the poor and helping the environment. I also want to be a vet when I grow up, so I'll be helping injured animals. Yes, I'm only one person, but a million begins with one.

LESLIE BRICENO ☀ AGE 15

Anne Frank

1929–1945 ◦ DIARIST ◦ GERMANY AND THE NETHERLANDS

Her voice was preserved out of the millions
that were silenced. . . . It has outlasted
the shouts of the murderers and has soared
above the voices of time.

—ERNST SCHNABEL, BIOGRAPHER

Anne looked around the dimly lit room. She and her family had been hiding from the Nazis for over two years, and they had to be extremely careful. Their hiding place was in a series of rooms over a warehouse. During the day they had to be completely silent, barely moving in their rooms and speaking only in tiny whispers, if at all. Any noise could mean discovery by the workers below. But Anne felt lucky that she had her family and a few friends hiding with her. Many Jews were not so lucky.

Anne tried to make her attic hiding place as nice as possible; she hung postcards and pictures of movie stars on the wall. But it wasn't really like home at all. The closest Anne could get to the outside world was to listen softly to the radio at night. But Anne had another way of escaping—her diary. In it, she wrote her thoughts, feelings, experiences, and dreams, leaving a treasured record of her life as a Jewish girl during the Holocaust.

Annelies Marie Frank was born on June 12, 1929, in Frankfurt, Germany. When Anne was just three years old, the Nazi Party gained control of her country. Their racist teachings called for the brutal oppression of Jews, and eventually, the Nazis sought to wipe the entire Jewish race off the face of the earth. By early 1934, Anne and her family had moved to Amsterdam, Holland, in an attempt to escape Nazi persecution.

Anne's father, Otto, started a new business, and things went well for a few years. But in 1940 the Germans took control of Amsterdam, and life for the Franks changed radically. In 1942 Anne's older sister was ordered to report to the Nazis so they could send her away to a concentration camp. The Franks knew families that had been sent to concentration camps, and none of them had ever been heard from again. The Frank family decided to go into hiding in a few rooms above Otto's business warehouse. They also hid another family and a friend. This was a risky choice, but they knew it was the only way the family could stay together. Anne was only thirteen years old.

When the Franks first escaped to their hiding place, they had to wear several outfits of clothing at once. Jews couldn't walk safely through the city streets with suitcases. Anne thought she would suffocate during that terrifying trip.

For the next two years, Anne and the others never dared to leave their hideout. They received food and other supplies from Dutch friends who risked their own lives by helping Jews. Anne often wrote in her beloved diary. She had been given the red-and-white-checkered journal for her thirteenth birthday, and it was one of the few things she was able to take with her into hiding. On September 28, 1942, Anne wrote: "So far you truly have been a great source of comfort to me . . . and now I can hardly wait for those moments when I'm able to write in you. Oh, I'm so glad I brought you along!"[22]

In August 1944, just after Anne's fifteenth birthday, an informant told the German police about the Franks' hiding place. Their hideout was raided, and everyone was arrested and sent to concentration camps. Of the eight people who hid above the warehouse, only Anne's father survived the horrifying ordeal. Anne died of typhoid in the Bergen-Belson concentration camp shortly before her sixteenth birthday.

When Anne's father returned to Amsterdam after the war, their brave Dutch friends gave him his daughter's diary. The Nazis had trashed the hideout during the raid, but the friends had managed to save Anne's book of memories. Otto Frank published his daughter's diary in 1947.

> Anne always dreamed of becoming a writer. She wrote short stories, fables, and essays. Anne's diary was translated into more than 30 languages and made into a Pulitzer Prize–winning play. In 1955, Anne's writings were adapted into a Broadway play called THE DIARY OF ANNE FRANK, and in the 1997 Broadway revival, the title character was played by another girl who rocked the world—Natalie Portman.

Today Anne's diary survives as the voice of an ordinary girl facing a horrible tragedy. Her words are proof of our capacity for courage and hope, even in the worst of times. On May 3, 1944, Anne wrote:

I've made up my mind to lead a different life from other girls . . . What I'm experiencing here is a good beginning to an interesting life, and that's the reason—the only reason—why I have to laugh at the humorous side of the most dangerous moments.[23]

The Nazis never crushed the spirit of this extraordinary girl. In one of her last diary entries, Anne writes, "I still believe in spite of everything, that people are truly good at heart."

HOW WILL YOU ROCK THE WORLD?

My dream is to become a writer. I want people to see things through my eyes...the eyes of a teen girl. I'm absolutely not going to write about the latest teen fashions or secret crushes. I'm not into that—I want to make a difference in people's lives.

LAURA DIVEGLIA ☼ AGE 13

Wilma Rudolph

1940–1994 ❁ ATHLETE ❁ UNITED STATES

I loved the feeling of freedom in running, the fresh air, the feeling that the only person I'm competing with is me.

—WILMA RUDOLPH

Nine-year-old Wilma hung back as the congregation filed into the church building. Almost everyone she knew in Clarksville was there. As her friends and family sat down in the pews, Wilma unbuckled the leg brace that she'd worn for years. Laying it aside, she took a deep breath and stepped through the church doors. Whispers rose as Wilma, who hadn't been seen without her brace since she was four years old, bravely walked down the aisle. As she took her seat, Wilma's pride mingled with the joy of the congregation. She had actually walked the full length of the church. Though her life would be filled with victories, today was one of Wilma's biggest triumphs. Little did the congregation dream that in days to come, this courageous girl would become known as the fastest woman in the world!

Wilma Rudolph was born on June 23, 1940, in St. Bethlehem, Tennessee. She was the twentieth of twenty-two children born to Ed and Blanche Rudolph. In her early childhood, Wilma battled measles, mumps, chicken pox, pneumonia, and scarlet fever. When she was four, she contracted polio, a crippling disease that left her unable to control the muscles in her left leg.

> Of her diagnosis, Wilma said, "The doctors told me I would never walk, but my mother told me I would, so I believed in my mother."

Wilma was told that she would never walk again, but she and her family refused to believe the diagnosis. Over the next ten years, they worked together to prove the doctors wrong. Wilma's brothers and sisters took turns massaging and exercising her leg every day. Twice a week, Wilma and her mother rode the bus to a hospital for physical therapy treatments that would strengthen her muscles. At that time, the southern United States was racially segregated, and the nearest hospital that accepted African Americans was fifty miles away in Nashville. Wilma and her mother were forced to ride in the back of the bus all the way.

With such a supportive family, Wilma made slow but encouraging progress. When she was six, her leg was strong enough that she could walk with the help of a special brace. This meant that she could finally go to school with her brothers and sisters. Wilma still couldn't participate in games and sports like the other kids did, however, so she was determined to get even stronger.

By the time Wilma was ten, she could walk short distances without the aid of her brace. Two years later, she joyfully mailed the brace back to the hospital in Nashville. She even began to play basketball! In the seventh grade, Wilma earned a spot on the school team, and over the next few years, she became a star player. During her sophomore year of high school, she scored a phenomenal 803 points in twenty-five games! This was a new record for Tennessee girls' basketball.

Wilma's amazing talent caught the attention of Ed Temple, a women's track coach from Tennessee State University. Temple was impressed with her speed and determination, and he invited her to attend a summer track program at Tennessee State. This gave her a wonderful opportunity to practice and improve her skills. And practice she did. In 1956 she was such a fast runner that she qualified for the United States Olympic track team! The Olympics were held in Melbourne, Australia, and young Wilma had barely traveled outside of Clarksville, Tennessee. She was thrilled! Only sixteen years old and the youngest member of the team, Wilma nevertheless won a bronze medal in the 400-meter relay.

Wilma resolved to compete in the next Olympics, and four years later, at the 1960 Olympic Games in Rome, she made history. With her stunning victories in the 100-meter dash, the 200-meter dash, and the 400-meter relay, Wilma became the first American woman runner to win three gold medals in one Olympics. She was officially dubbed the fastest woman in the world.

Wilma received many other prestigious awards for her incredible athletic skill. She was voted Woman Athlete of the Year by the Associated Press and was named Sportsman of the Year by a group of European sportswriters. By the time she retired from track in 1962, she had won the James E. Sullivan Award for outstanding amateur athlete and the Babe Didrikson Zaharias Award, an honor bestowed on the best female athletes in the world.

In 1963 Wilma graduated from Tennessee State University with a degree in elementary education. She became a schoolteacher, track coach, and director of children's sports programs. In 1967 she joined Operation Champ, an organization of athletes who coached inner-city children and teens. In the late 1970s Wilma founded her own company, Wilma Unlimited, and traveled around the country giving inspirational speeches. She shared her own story of triumph and encouraged kids to pursue their dreams no matter what obstacles they faced. Wilma was

When Wilma returned to her hometown after her Olympic victories, she was greeted by cheers and banners. The town even held a parade in her honor. The parade, attended by both African American and white citizens, was the first integrated event in Clarksville's history!

passionate about encouraging young athletes, and in 1981 she founded the Wilma Rudolph Foundation to train young people in sports.

Biographer Tom Biracree wrote:

Wilma Rudolph had overcome polio and risen from poverty to become the "fastest woman in the world." She had won respect for women in the male-dominated world of sports, through her own spectacular achievements. Yet, Rudolph told [a] journalist that she valued her own idealism as much as any of her unique accomplishments: "I just want to be remembered as a hardworking lady with certain beliefs." [24]

In 1994 Wilma Rudolph died of a brain tumor. A gifted athlete and a determined competitor, she inspired many with her remarkable courage and talent. Her life is an inspiration to everyone who has a dream that seems impossible. Wilma's triumphs prove that with determination and vision, even the most devastating setbacks can be overcome.

ROCK ON!

JESSICA WATSON

Sixteen-year-old Jessica Watson dreamed for four years of sailing solo, nonstop around the world. When she finally guided her yacht out of Sydney Harbour in November 2009, she knew she was taking on the most challenging task of her life so far. Over the next seven months, Jessica dealt with violent storms, turbulent seas, and disheartening loneliness until she returned to a hero's welcome the following May. Jessica's trip has inspired many others to take up sailing, and in 2011 Jessica won the Young Australian of the Year Award.

The Night Witches

1941–1945 ❀ FIGHTER PILOTS ❀ RUSSIA

*Even if it were possible to gather and place at your feet
all the flowers on earth, this would not constitute
sufficient tribute to your valor.*

—FRENCH WWII PILOTS, PRAISING THE NIGHT WITCHES

Marina looked out the plane's window and could see the dark forest below her. They were dropping fast, and there was no place to land. The snowstorm raged around them, weighting their wings down with heavy ice and dragging them closer and closer to death.

"Lighten the plane!" yelled Valentina, who was struggling to maintain their altitude. Marina and Polina opened the hatch in the floor and threw out anything that wasn't bolted down. But it was no use—the plane kept plunging toward the trees. When they had set out to beat a flight record, they never imagined they'd be fighting for their lives.

The Night Witches
were not the first
Soviet warrior women.
The legendary Amazons
were also from
southern Russia!

Suddenly, the snowstorm was *inside* the plane as well as outside. Valentina and Polina turned to see Marina standing above the open hatch, with a fierce look on her face. She was wearing a parachute. "Don't do it, Marina! We'll never find you again in this wilderness!" they yelled. But it was too late—Marina threw herself out into the cold, dark night.

With the lighter load, they managed to keep the plane aloft until they found a clearing to land in, close to a village. Marina's remarkable courage had saved their lives. But after days of searching, they couldn't find her. She must have died alone in the woods, they figured. Ten days later, long after they and the Russian public had given up hope, a surprised hunter stumbled across Marina, freezing and half-starved, in the desolate forest.

The Winged Sisters received a heroes' welcome when they returned to Moscow. Tens of thousands of fans lined the streets to cheer the winners of the women's world record for a distance flight after their dangerous six-thousand-kilometer journey across Russia. Each pilot was awarded the Hero of the Soviet Union Gold Star—the first women to earn such an honor. But the crowds really came to see Captain Marina Raskova, the brave young woman who risked her life to save their mission.

Marina was just nineteen when she began flying and was the first woman in Russia to pass the navigator exam. She inspired thousands of girls, factory workers and even housewives, to earn their wings after her heroic 1938 flight. She was the Amelia Earhart of Russia. Local flying clubs were set up by the government to train girls as young as seventeen, free of charge. Marina encouraged an entire generation of Russian girls to push themselves, to see what they could do . . . girls who would soon be called on to help save their homeland from the coming war.

American women weren't
allowed to fly in combat
until 1993, 50 years
after World War II and
the Night Witches!

In June 1941 Adolf Hitler surprised Russia and the world when he launched Operation Barbarossa, a sneak attack against the Soviet air force. German bombers destroyed squadrons of Soviet planes as they sat parked on their airfields. The unprovoked airstrikes not only threw the Soviet Union into chaos but also gave the Germans complete air superiority. Much of the Soviet Union's air force was destroyed in the attack; the country was in trouble.

The Soviet people were eager to defend themselves against this attack on their *Rodina* (Mother Russia). Recruits poured in, including thousands of teenage girls who had plenty of flying experience and wanted to get to the front. At first, these girl pilots were rejected. One official's response to a girl's application was: "Things may be bad, but we're not so desperate that we're going to put little girls like you up in the skies. Go home and help your mother."[25]

> In June 1943 a ship was built by the United States and given to the Russians to use in the war effort. The Americans named the ship the SS MARINA RASKOVA, in memory of the heroic Soviet pilot.

But it wasn't long before Russian officials changed their tune; there simply weren't enough male pilots and crews left in Russia to challenge the Germans.

Again, it was Marina Raskova to the rescue. Promoted to major in the Soviet Air Force, she convinced the high command to let her recruit and train all female combat units. On Radio Moscow, Marina asked for female volunteers to fight on the front lines with the men. The response was overwhelming—who wouldn't want to serve under their hero? Bags of applications arrived every day, and Marina personally interviewed thousands of hopefuls. In the end more than a thousand of the best candidates were chosen. Some got to be fighter pilots, others navigators, and the rest mechanics and support personnel. Most of the young women chosen for the elite units were still teenagers!

From the very beginning, these girls faced different obstacles than their male counterparts. The government didn't even bother to make women's uniforms and instead gave them the same uniforms as the men.

One female fighter remembered, "They were gigantic . . . vests dangled down below the knee, trousers hitched up almost to the chin . . . coats spilled onto the floor like . . . bridal trains." Another said, "God knows what the Germans would have thought." And since the battle against the Germans was already underway, their training was accelerated, to say the least. The young women had to cram nearly three years of flying experience into just three months!

The most serious difficulty they faced, however, was the sexism of their male comrades. Many male pilots refused to fly with women "wingmen" or to go up in airplanes that had been repaired by women mechanics. Many believed that women weren't as skilled or as brave as men and had no place in the war.

The female fighters didn't let these attitudes stop them, however. The Germans had invaded their country too, and they knew they had the skills to fight back. It didn't take long for the women to prove themselves. Like male pilots, they battled in countless aerial dogfights, bombed bridges and ammunition depots, cleared safe paths for advancing Russian soldiers, and protected Soviet military installations.

They were particularly successful in their night bombing attacks on advancing German troops. Sleep was critical for exhausted soldiers on the front lines, so the all-night terror of the Night Witches' attacks was devastating to the enemy. A German commander described the effect of their raids: "We simply couldn't grasp that the Soviet airmen that caused us the greatest trouble were in fact WOMEN. These women feared nothing. They came night after night . . . and . . . wouldn't give us any sleep at all."[26] In one evening, the pilots attacked eighteen times! The Germans were so afraid of the raids, they dubbed the pilots Night Witches.

The night attacks were almost as terrifying for the pilots as well. They flew in biplanes that were normally used just for training, since they were very slow and could be seen and heard from a great distance. They were easy targets for the enemy. One female pilot tells of a particularly terrifying mission:

The antiaircraft guns fired at us fiercely from all directions, and suddenly I felt our aircraft hit. My left foot slipped down into an empty

space below me; the bottom of the cockpit had been shot away. I felt
something hot streaming down my left arm and leg—I was wounded.
Blinded by the searchlights . . . I was completely disoriented: the sky
and earth were indistinguishable to my vision . . . [27]

The flimsy planes were made of canvas, so if shot they often went
up in flames. This meant almost certain death for the crew, since there
were no parachutes on board! Even if they managed to land the plane,
they had to be careful to land on the *Russian* side of the battle lines,
so they would not to be taken prisoner by the enemy.

The Night Witches devised risky tactics to make up for their planes.
In one maneuver, a brave pilot would fly alone over the enemy camp,
attracting their floodlights and machine gun fire. As the Germans shot
at the lone plane, two more pilots would glide in with their engines off
and drop their bombs. Before the Germans knew what had happened,
all three planes were gone. If a much faster German plane came after
them, their only escape was to outmaneuver it. They often did this by
flying so low to the ground so that their planes were hidden by trees!
Night Witches were so difficult to catch, in fact, that German pilots
were promised an Iron Cross (the German medal of highest honor) for
shooting one down.

These courageous female pilots saw at least as much action as the
men: in just one all-female unit, the pilots flew in over twenty-four
thousand combat assaults during the war! They won thousands of medals and honors. In fact, twenty-nine female pilots won the prestigious
Hero of the Soviet Union award; twenty-three of those awards went to
Night Witches!

One daredevil pilot, in particular, became quite famous to the
Russian public, and infamous to her German enemies—Lilya Litvak.
When she was just fifteen, Lily, as she was known, tried to join her local
flying club, but was told that she would have to wait two more years like
everyone else. But Lily was determined and read every aviation book she
could get her hands on. She pestered instructors, displaying her incredible knowledge, until they gave in and let her enroll early, at age sixteen.
Lily was a natural flier, and learned much faster than other students.
Soon this teenager was so good she, too, became an instructor.

When Marina made her radio announcement for female pilots, Lily was one of the first girls to sign up for the all-female units. She was quickly promoted to fight in the dangerous battles over Stalingrad with an all-male unit. Although Lily was extremely beautiful, she didn't let that distract her male comrades from their mission. When one young fighter confessed his love for Lily, she replied, "Let's get the fighting over first, darling—then maybe we can talk about love, eh?"

Lily quickly earned the respect of her male squad. In less than a year of combat, she flew 168 successful missions and shot down an astounding twelve enemy planes. In recognition of her bravery, she was awarded the prestigious Order of the Red Banner and was promoted to senior lieutenant. She painted a large white rose on each side of her cockpit, plus a row of twelve smaller roses along the nose for each plane she shot down, earning her the name the White Rose of Stalingrad. When German fighters saw the White Rose coming, they would usually turn and flee rather than fight. Over the radio, the Soviets could hear German pilots call warnings to each other as she approached, "*Achtung, Litvak!*"

Once Lily shot down a German plane, and the pilot parachuted out and was captured by Russian troops. When they questioned the highly decorated Nazi, he asked to meet the pilot who had shot him down. He was surprised and angry when Lily walked in, and he demanded an explanation for this Russian joke. But his anger turned to humiliation when Lily began describing their dogfight in detail, explaining exactly how she had beaten him. The German could not even look at her. "Her eyes were flashing like a tiger. She was enjoying herself," said a friend who was there.

Sadly, in August 1943, Lily's luck ran out. While scouting the front lines for enemy bombers, a group of German fighters distracted the other Russian

It was almost impossible for female pilots to wash their hair on the freezing front lines. But Lily came up with a brilliant plan: after a day of flying, she opened her plane's radiator and drained scalding water into a bucket. Right on the runway, she'd fling off her helmet and soap up with the only hot water to be found!

planes as eight fighters ganged up on Lily. They had seen the White Rose and weren't about to let her escape again. She fought back with all she had, and it took all eight German planes to hit her, but the White Rose of Stalingrad finally went down in flames. Lily was just twenty-two years old when she died.

Marina Raskova also died before the end of the war. In 1943, while leading two planes through a blinding snowstorm, Marina became disoriented and flew too low. She crashed into the steep bank of the Volga River and died. The female fighter pilots had seen many of their friends killed in battle, but losing their inspiration, their hero, was almost more than they could bear. One pilot described the reaction to Marina's death: "There was a moment or two of complete silence. . . . Then it seemed that everyone was crying together. . . . All around was the sound of the most anguished sobbing."[28]

Although many of Russia's greatest war heroines didn't live to see their country defeat the German invaders, their courage and contributions are still celebrated. After the war, a monument was built near where Lily's plane went down to honor her as a war hero. And in 1990 Lily was still remembered by the Russian people when she finally received the Hero of the Soviet Union award from then-prime minister Mikhail Gorbachev. Marina and Lily would've been proud of their women comrades. The female combat units took part in some of the heaviest, most dangerous air combat in history. They refused to back down, and they helped fight off the German invasion and win the war.

> In spite of her tough exterior, Lily loved beauty. She picked wildflowers before missions, tucking them behind her ears for good luck. Even on the day she was shot down, Lily had flowers pinned to her control panel

> Lily knew her parents wouldn't approve of her flying, so she told them she joined the drama club and had practice after school.

HOW WILL YOU ROCK THE WORLD?

I want to create a stunt for planes. I will perform the stunt, along with risky turns and maneuvers, better than any other pilot. I also want to be the first pilot to test out new jets. I think flying is the best thing in the world and that's how I plan to rock it.

LEIGH DELAHANTY · AGE 12

Temple Grandin

1947– ⚛ SCIENTIST, INVENTOR, AND ADVOCATE ⚛ UNITED STATES

*I do believe that recognizing different capacities
and kinds of thought and expression can lead to greater
connectedness and understanding.*

—TEMPLE GRANDIN

Temple galloped across the ranch. Her breath exploded out in great gasps; her heart raced like it might fly out of her chest. She felt like she was having a heart attack, but she couldn't stop. She couldn't slow down. She couldn't think. She had to keep moving. Moving. Moving.

Temple was having a panic attack. She had them all the time, and each attack was terrifying. This time, as Temple raced around her Aunt Ann's ranch, she caught sight of something out of the corner of her eye. *The squeeze chute!* she thought desperately. She pictured cows standing in the machine as workers gave them shots. At first the cattle were nervous, but once the side gates closed in and squeezed their flanks to hold them in place, the animals relaxed.

In 1943 Dr. Leo Kanner first coined the term autism to describe the unusual behavior of children he was working with. Autism is a brain disorder diagnosed in early childhood. Some classic symptoms include poor speech and eye contact; appearance of deafness; tantrums; lack of interest in people; and repetitive behaviors (like rocking, spinning, or hand flapping). The cause of autism is still unknown and, while early intervention and treatment has been shown to help, there is no known cure.

Before anyone could stop her, Temple threw herself into the empty chute. Down on all fours, she called out, "Pull the lever!"

Aunt Ann had no idea what Temple was doing, but she pulled the lever anyway. The gates closed in, squeezing Temple with a gentle pressure. Relief came instantly. She could feel her panic drifting away. Her breathing slowed. Her heartbeat slowed. A wave of calm swept over her. It was like a miracle.

Temple knew she had to build a squeeze machine of her own.

That summer, seventeen-year-old Temple Grandin did indeed design and build her own squeeze machine, which gave her great relief from the overwhelming anxiety caused by her autism. This was Temple's first important step in turning her disability to an asset that would eventually help her achieve her dreams.

When Temple Grandin was born in Boston, Massachusetts, in 1947, no one knew she had autism. Although as a baby she struggled whenever she was held and preferred being alone in the baby carriage, Temple's parents had no idea she was unusual. As she grew into a toddler, however, they noticed that she didn't talk, and they worried she might be deaf. They also noticed she didn't play like other children her age. While the toddler next door built sand castles with friends and played patty-cake with her mother, Temple spent hours alone watching sand trickle through her fingers, mesmerized by each individual grain. Temple was different.

When Temple was two and a half, a doctor diagnosed her with brain damage. Back then almost no one knew about autism. People with Temple's symptoms were usually forced to live in a hospital or mental institution, away from their families. That's what the doctor recommended for Temple, but her mother refused. Instead she started Temple in a speech therapy class and hired a nanny to work with Temple and her sister every day. "I would tune out," Temple said, describing her early years, "shut off my ears, and daydream." The teachers brought her back to earth. With their help, Temple began to talk and interact with her family.

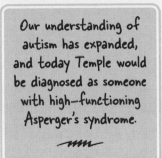

Our understanding of autism has expanded, and today Temple would be diagnosed as someone with high-functioning Asperger's syndrome.

When Temple hit adolescence, however, life got more difficult. People with autism often experience intensified symptoms during the teen years, probably triggered by hormonal changes. For Temple, it was crippling panic attacks. She was also teased a lot more for the unusual way she talked and acted.

Fortunately, in high school Temple met one of her most influential mentors: Mr. Carlock, her science teacher. He could see that Temple was incredibly bright, but it was also clear that her brain worked differently than other students' did. Temple learned visually; she saw the world in pictures. While other kids teased her for being different, Carlock encouraged Temple to use those differences to her benefit. He suggested she design experiments that used her unique visual talents. Temple took his advice and began to think and experiment like a scientist. "He spent hours giving me encouragement when I became dejected by all the teasing by classmates. Mr. Carlock's science lab was a refuge from a world I did not understand."

Throughout Temple's childhood, her mother pushed her to do things she was uncomfortable with, to stretch herself, and to find and develop her passions. In high school, when Temple's panic attacks were nearly nonstop, her mother forced her to spend the summer at her Aunt Ann's ranch in Arizona. It

Temple got kicked out of her first high school after she threw a book at a girl who was teasing her.

Here's how Temple describes the workings of her brain: "I think in pictures. Words are like a second language to me. I translate both spoken and written words into full-color movies, complete with sound, which run like a VCR tape in my head."

~~~

turned out to be one of the best moves of Temple's life. At the ranch, she spent her time helping with the animals and designing things. After she discovered that pressure from the cattle chute could relieve her anxiety for hours at a time, Temple designed and built one of her own. Temple describes the effects of using the machine: "I felt very calm and serene.... This was the first time I ever felt really comfortable in my own skin."

On the ranch, Temple had another important breakthrough—she discovered her love of cattle. She realized she had the ability to picture the world through their eyes. She could envision what the cows were seeing, how they were feeling, and predict how that would affect their behavior. Cattle and their behavior soon became Temple's passion. During college, she studied psychology and designed a study of human stress relief using her squeeze machine on classmates.

For her master's degree, Temple moved to Arizona where she could be near Aunt Ann and the ranch. At Arizona State University she studied animal science, focusing on cattle and feedlot systems. When she asked to do her master's thesis on the behavior of cattle in different types of cattle chutes, her adviser thought she was crazy and said no. But Temple wouldn't take no for an answer. She found two new advisers, in the Construction and Design Departments, and began her survey. She discovered that some types of chutes were more likely to injure cattle, some types of cattle were

Early in Temple's career, a man blocked her from entering a feedlot, saying, "No girls allowed." So Temple dressed as a man in heavy overalls, a hardhat, and sunglasses and got through with no problem.

~~~

more accident-prone, and that a certain timing for operation was ideal for reducing stress and injury. Today, her findings are widely used by the cattle industry.

Once out of school, Temple had to work even harder to get people to trust and believe in her abilities. Temple wanted to design better equipment for feedlots—equipment that wouldn't scare cattle, that would keep them calm and reduce injuries and unnecessary deaths. Temple wanted to design a better life for the millions of cattle in these facilities. But in the 1960s almost no women worked in feedlots. There certainly weren't any women with autism.

One of Temple's first livestock design projects was a dip vat for John Wayne's Red River feed yard in Arizona. A dip vat is a long, narrow, deep pool filled with pesticide that cattle swim through to get rid of ticks, lice, and other parasites. Temple didn't like the existing designs. The steep, slick ramps often caused cattle to panic as they entered the pool. Some flipped over and drowned. Temple's redesign had a more gradual ramp with grooves to give the cattle better footing.

The cowboys who worked at the feed yard, however, didn't believe Temple knew what she was doing. Before the first test of her new design, the cowboys covered her ramp with a metal sheet, converting it back into the slippery system she was trying to fix. The first day they used it, the cattle panicked, as they had before, and two

> Temple wrote, "From as far back as I can remember, I always hated to be hugged. I wanted to experience the good feeling of being hugged, but it was just too overwhelming.... When I was six, I would wrap myself up in blankets and get under sofa cushions, because the pressure was relaxing. I used to daydream for hours ... about constructing a device that would apply pressure to my body."

> One third of all cattle and hogs in the United States are now handled in more humane facilities designed by Temple.

> Temple's favorite TV show is STAR TREK. She identifies with Spock and Data, describing herself as a "pure logical being." Human emotions often baffle her, just as they did the Vulcan and the android.
>
> ~~~

flipped over in the pool and drowned. When Temple found out, she was furious! After she insisted they remove the metal sheet, the cowboys were amazed that the ramp worked perfectly. The cattle entered the pool calmly and no more drowned.

Temple went on to design and redesign feedlots all across America. She has written countless articles in industry magazines explaining how to improve animal facilities. Temple has her doctorate in animal science, works as a professor at Colorado State University, and is considered a world-famous expert on the behavior and psychology of cattle and hogs, as well as an advocate for their humane treatment.

She is also a world-famous expert on autism. Temple believes that intervening early and encouraging the talents of people with autism are the keys to helping them lead a happier, more fulfilling life. Through her bestselling books and frequent appearances, Temple has helped thousands of people with autism.

In 2010 *Time Magazine* listed Temple in its one hundred Most Influential People, and that same year a movie about her life won seven Emmy awards. The squeeze chute Temple invented as a teenager is now called a hug box and provides anxiety relief to people with autism all around the world. Temple used it herself for forty-five years until she didn't need it anymore. "I'm into hugging people now," she has stated.

Despite all the challenges Temple has faced because of her differences, she is clear about not wishing to change. She believes her disabilities gave her unique abilities. "If I could snap my fingers and be nonautistic, I would not. Autism is part of what I am."

HOW WILL YOU ROCK THE WORLD?

I'd offer a summer horse camp for children with autism. I would call it Camp Horse Sense. There they would learn a little bit more about the horses, like how to tack and untack the horses, how to trot and canter, and possibly how to jump. I would be giving back to the world by teaching children how to be kind, loving, and caring toward other creatures. Letting children learn how to be independent and gentle with such large animals will be a great way to let children express themselves and feel good and free.

CATHERINE SOUTH ☼ AGE 13

Susan Eloise (S. E.) Hinton

APPROXIMATELY 1948– ⚬ NOVELIST ⚬ UNITED STATES

When I was young, girls never got to DO anything.
They got to rat their hair and outline
their eyes in black, but that was about the
extent of their activities.

—S. E. HINTON

Susan Hinton watched as actor Matt Dillon performed a scene taken from her novel *Tex*. She still couldn't believe that her book was going to become a movie. Her teenage fans had demanded it—they wrote so many letters to producers, begging that they make the movie, that Hollywood finally listened. Other movies followed, like *Rumble Fish*; *That Was Then, This Is Now*; and one based on Susan's most famous novel, *The Outsiders*, which was directed by Francis Ford Coppola and starred Matt Dillon, Emilio Estevez, Ralph Macchio, Patrick Swayze, and Tom Cruise.

Susan was very involved in the process of turning her books into movies. She wanted everything to be right, so she helped with many aspects of the productions. As a fifteen-year-old girl writing her first novel, *The Outsiders*, Susan never imagined that she would be published, that her stories would become some of the most popular books for teens ever, or that she would help turn them into movies.

Susan Eloise Hinton was born in Tulsa, Oklahoma, around 1948. As a child, she loved to read, and she dreamed about becoming a writer. Her first writings were about cowboys and horses. Susan's father died when she was in high school. She was close to him, and as he got sicker and sicker, she turned more and more to her writing.

While attending Will Rogers High School, Susan wrote *The Outsiders*. She began her first draft when she was just fifteen, and by the time the novel was published in 1967, she had rewritten the book four times! In her late teens, Susan became an overnight success. Unlike most other books at the time, her novel dealt with the reality of life for many teenagers. Although some people criticized the book for being too violent, most praised it for its true-to-life depiction of teen conflict.

The Outsiders tells the story of Ponyboy Curtis and his greaser friends as they fight against the socs (short for *socials*) and struggle to find their place in the world. Susan got her inspiration for the book from witnessing the real conflict between greasers and socs in her own hometown. She was bothered by the way many of her peers judged each other solely by appearance and income.

Susan's novel was immediately popular with teens, and the critics gave it rave reviews. Her early success put a great deal of pressure on her, and she suffered from writer's block for several years. Susan began to wonder if *The Outsiders* had just been a fluke. However, three years later she began writing again. After receiving a degree in education from the University of Tulsa in 1971, Susan published her second novel. *That Was Then, This Is Now*

The film THE OUTSIDERS is dedicated to the students and librarians who requested that the book be made into a movie.

~~~

is also about teen conflict, violence, and troubled homes. Susan continued to work with this theme, publishing *Rumble Fish* in 1975, *Tex* in 1979, and *Taming the Star Runner* in 1988. All of her novels were well-received, and four were made into successful movies.

> The same year THE OUTSIDERS was published, Susan received a D in her creative writing class!

Susan's first four novels were written in the first person, with a boy narrating the story. She said she *became* the narrator as she told the story and felt more comfortable writing from a boy's perspective. This may be because boys were some of her closest friends while growing up. She used her initials, S. E., while writing her books because when she published *The Outsiders*, she didn't want readers to know she was a girl. She was afraid that no one would believe that a girl could really know anything about gangs, abusive parents, or peer pressure from a boy's point of view.

Susan's novels are still read and enjoyed by millions of teenagers each year. She's also written children's books. Her picture book *Big David, Little David* and chapter book *The Puppy Sister* were published in the mid-1990s. Susan's books have won countless awards, such as the American Library Association's Best Books for Young Adults and the School Library Journal's Best Books of the Year. Susan was also the first recipient of the Margaret A. Edwards Award for her success in reaching her young adult audience. Susan was one of the first authors to write realistically about the conflicts and concerns of teens. Her style has influenced the genre of young adult literature forever.

ROCK ON!

NANCY YI FAN

When eleven-year-old Nancy Yi Fan started writing her novel *Swordbird*, she'd only been speaking English for four years. She and her family had moved to the United States from Beijing, China, when Nancy was seven years old, and she relied on books and her love of reading to learn the language. Nancy sent *Swordbird* to publishers when she was thirteen and had a contract before she knew it! *Swordbird* was a *New York Times* bestseller and was later published in a bilingual Chinese/English edition. Nancy's second book, *Sword Quest*, came out when she was fifteen.

AdRiaNa OcamPo

1955– ☉ PLANETARY GEOLOGIST
COLOMBIA, ARGENTINA, UNITED STATES

*I think you never stop learning when you are a scientist
and you are being constantly challenged to find new solutions,
new ways of thinking.*

—ADRIANA OCAMPO

A driana sat on the bleachers among the sprawling crowd of
five hundred thousand people. She and the other members of
Space Exploration Post 509—an aerospace engineering club for
teens in Pasadena, California—had traveled all the way across the
country to witness this historic event: the launching of *Apollo 17*,
the sixth and final human mission to the Moon. They had fund-
raised and worked at NASA's Jet Propulsion Lab (JPL) to earn money
for the trip, and they were starting to get nervous that all their efforts
might be wasted. The launch was planned for 9:53 PM, but the rocket
engines had gone silent just thirty seconds before then. Now the

anxious crowd had been waiting for over two hours since the scheduled time for liftoff.

As Adriana and her friends were beginning to wonder if liftoff would happen at all, the engines grumbled to life. At about half past midnight, the spacecraft launched with a force that made the ground tremble, and Adriana watched as a fiery plume made the night sky almost as bright as day. She followed *Apollo 17*'s path into space, and as she had many times before, she wondered about what lay beyond the Earth's atmosphere. What did other planets look like? What were they made of? Could we travel there? Did they support life of their own? Adriana had always been interested in space science, and as she watched *Apollo 17* disappear into the darkness, she again resolved to build her interests into a career that would let her explore these questions for the rest of her life.

Adriana Ocampo was born in Colombia, South America, on January 5, 1955. Before her first birthday, Adriana's family moved to Argentina, where she lived until she was fourteen. Growing up, Adriana was fascinated by science; she especially enjoyed looking up at the stars, and she dreamed of traveling into space. On July 20, 1969, she and her family crowded around their television set with neighbors and friends to watch coverage of the first Moon landing. Adriana was transfixed by the images on the screen. In December of that same year, Adriana moved to Southern California in the United States.

Adriana's new home offered many opportunities to pursue her interests in space and science. Soon after she moved, she joined Space Exploration Post 509, a science group that met at NASA's nearby Jet Propulsion Lab (JPL) and worked on projects ranging from robots and circuit boards to rockets and weather stations. During her junior year of high school, she got a part-time job at the JPL, and after high school graduation, she continued to work there while studying for a college degree. When she was only nineteen, she convinced the JPL to fund a weather station project she'd been working on with a team of friends from Post 509. There was tough competition for JPL funds, and

Adriana used to borrow items from the kitchen and her father's workshop to build a lunar colony.

the group had won an honor given to only the most promising of ideas and proposals.

After college, Adriana started working full time at the JPL, where she participated in many groundbreaking projects. One of her early assignments was to help analyze images of Mars that had been taken by two probes during NASA's Viking mission. The Viking project sought to explore the

> Adriana's expeditions in southern Mexico and Belize revealed rocks that had launched from the Crater of Doom and landed up to 200 miles away.

makeup of the planet and its atmosphere and to search for evidence of life. As part of her work, Adriana also coordinated observations of the two Martian moons and helped develop a map of one of those moons, Phobos. In a later mission called the Observer project, Adriana was to run a heat-sensing machine that would further determine the composition of Mars and help scientists make better maps of the planet. Unfortunately, though, scientists lost communication with the Observer three days before it was scheduled to go into orbit around Mars. Other spacecrafts have since been sent to the planet, and a few have landed successfully. Though Adriana has taken on many other projects, she continues to be interested and involved in these missions.

Beyond Mars, Adriana has participated in missions to study Jupiter and the outer planets. She studied information sent back from the two *Voyager* spacecrafts about Jupiter and its moons, information which surprisingly showed evidence of volcanic activity on the moon Io. She also helped guide the *Voyager* spacecraft toward Saturn, from which they would continue on to Uranus and Neptune and then beyond all the planets in our solar system.

Another mission, the *Galileo*, allowed for more exploration of Jupiter and its moons. Adriana was particularly involved in coordinating *Galileo*'s near-infrared technology, which was designed to gather information about Jupiter's clouds and composition as well as the temperatures of the planet. Adriana focused special attention on one of Jupiter's moons, Europa. Images of Europa suggested that its icy surface may have been an ocean at one time, or even that an ocean may currently exist under Europa's frozen crust. This discovery prompted scientists to redirect the Europa-bound *Galileo* into Jupiter's atmosphere, where they knew it would be destroyed. They wanted to protect any potential water on Europa from contamination by Earth-based materials.

In addition to studying other planets, Adriana is also interested in geology on our own planet Earth, and she has made exciting discoveries here too. At a conference in 1988, she noticed a ring of cenotes, or sinkholes, near the Yucatán Peninsula in Mexico. Adriana believed this pattern might suggest an enormous impact crater from an asteroid colliding with Earth sometime in the past. She and other scientists have since looked into this theory more closely, and many believe that a large asteroid did crash into Earth at that spot sixty-five million years ago, at the end of the age of dinosaurs. In fact, Adriana and other scientists think that this asteroid may be the reason that dinosaurs became extinct. The impact of this huge asteroid would likely have caused fires, earthquakes, and massive tidal waves, and sent a thick layer of dirt, dust, vapor, and smoke in the air. Scientists theorize that the Earth would have become dark and cold for an extended time, and many species would not have survived. The asteroid impact site has been named the Chicxulub crater, sometimes referred to as the Crater of Doom.

While Adriana continues her pioneering work in planetary geology, she also spends time promoting science education and bringing scientists together on an international level. She founded a course in planetary sciences that has been held all around the world in countries including Mexico, Costa Rica, Nigeria, Egypt, Jordan, and China. Adriana is active in encouraging young people to pursue science through such organizations as the United States Society of Hispanic Professional Engineers and the Society of Women Engineers. She has taken her own education seriously, as well, following up her bachelor's degree with a master's degree in 1997 and starting work on a PhD soon after. She has been an executive in NASA's international space science program and has also worked for the European Space Agency in the Netherlands. Starting in the early 1990s, Adriana organized the Space Conference of the Americas, which has brought together people from many nations to discuss and learn about space science.

Adriana has been widely recognized for her accomplishments. Among other honors, she has earned the JPL Advisory Council for Women Award and has been named Woman of the Year in Science by Comisión Femenil, an organization that promotes the empowerment of Hispanic women. In 2003 she was named one of the 50 most important women in science by *Discover* magazine.

Adriana's enthusiasm and expertise have helped her succeed both as a scientist and as someone who shares her work and passion with others. As she continues to pursue the career she's dreamed about since childhood, Adriana will undoubtedly gain further admiration and make more exciting discoveries about Earth and other planets.

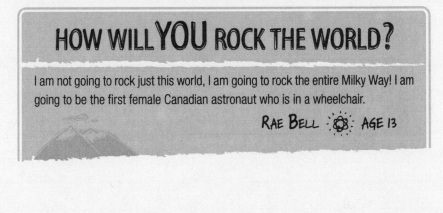

HOW WILL YOU ROCK THE WORLD?

I am not going to rock just this world, I am going to rock the entire Milky Way! I am going to be the first female Canadian astronaut who is in a wheelchair.

RAE BELL ☼ AGE 13

AmatalRauf al-ShaRki (Raufa Hassan)

1958–2011 ◈ JOURNALIST AND ACTIVIST ◈ YEMEN

Inside me I didn't like that veil anymore. I felt it was a big lie...
I wanted to be me. Just me, accepted the way I was.... I began to
realise that the veil was just something to hold me back in life and
not really for my benefit. Since then this started to rage inside
me.... I had become a different person.

—RAUFA HASSAN

I t was 1975, and television had just come to the country of Yemen.
Seventeen-year-old Amatalrauf al-Sharki, famous with the Yemeni
public as radio personality Raufa Hassan, was about to appear in one
of the first Yemeni television programs. After all, Raufa had been the
star of her own successful radio show since she was twelve. But this was
entirely different—for the first time, her country would see her. And she
had quite a surprise for them.

Raufa had just returned from her first year of college and had vowed to stop wearing her traditional veil. It was the custom of most Muslim women, especially in Yemen, to wear the veil in public at all times to conceal themselves from the view of men. While Raufa went to college in the less traditional country of Egypt, she came to believe that the veil was a symbol that held women back from achieving equality. To her, it was a form of discrimination. If she wore it, Raufa would feel she was lying to herself and her country. She wouldn't do it.

When the cameras began rolling, all of Yemen saw the face of their favorite female celebrity. Many viewers were shocked, including Raufa's family and friends, but Raufa stood by her beliefs. By not wearing a veil, Raufa publicly asserted her independence and began a personal campaign to promote women's rights in Islamic countries.

Amatalrauf al-Sharki was born in 1958 in a North Yemen town called Ibb. By the time she was in the sixth grade, she had begun her work in the media. Her first job was singing in a children's radio show, but she quickly moved on to bigger things. One day, a broadcaster didn't show up for his program at the radio station, and Amatalrauf agreed to fill in for him. The twelve-year-old girl did such a good job as his replacement that she was asked to be an official broadcaster with her own show!

However, Amatalrauf was sure that her father would be angry if she had her own radio show. He would consider it a scandal if his daughter were publicly speaking over the airwaves. But Amatalrauf was determined to have her own show, so she and the other station employees worked out a way for her to continue on the radio. She simply changed her broadcasting name so that no one would know who she was. Amatalrauf did tell her mother, who saw no real harm in the idea and was happy that her daughter would be earning an income. From that day on, Amatalrauf became known to the Yemeni public as Raufa Hassan.

Each day, Raufa would go to the radio station after school to record her broadcasts. Her plan worked well until six months later, when an announcer accidentally introduced her as "Raufa Hassan *al-Sharki*." Her secret identity was ruined! Raufa's father threatened to keep her from working anymore, but he eventually backed down and allowed Raufa to continue her show.

Raufa's broadcasts were different from most. For three years she had a program about family topics. While other such programs dealt with women's household duties as a wife, Raufa emphasized that family responsibilities belong to both men *and* women. Even as a teen, she promoted equality between the sexes.

As of 2009, the illiteracy rate of Yemeni women had dropped to an estimated 55 percent.[29]

Over the next few years, Raufa became more involved in the women's movement, participating in activities and organizations that advocated women's rights. She was active in the Yemeni Women's Association until a religious group shut it down in 1973. That same year, at age fifteen, she and three friends founded a school to teach Yemeni girls and women to read and write. This was a major step for education in Yemen, where over 70 percent of the women were illiterate. Raufa also shocked the public when she marched in a Yemeni military parade. She and a group of girls trained for three weeks, learning how to walk in formation and carry guns. They were the first women to participate in the Revolution Day celebration, previously an all-male activity.

But perhaps Raufa's most significant actions centered around the question of whether or not to wear a veil. Like most other Yemeni women, she was brought up with the tradition of covering her face except for her eyes. During her radio broadcasts, though, she couldn't wear a veil because it would muffle her voice. Raufa decided to keep this a secret; she knew it would be offensive to many people— especially her family—if they knew she performed her broadcasts without a veil. Only the people at the station knew about it, and she didn't even let many of them see her face uncovered. During her five years at the station, only the program producer and the station engineer were allowed to watch while she recorded her broadcasts. Inside, though, Raufa was becoming more and more uncomfortable with wearing her veil. She began to see it as a device that held her back as a woman.

In 1975 Raufa graduated from high school. Despite opposition from her family, she attended Cairo University in Egypt, where she studied

In 2010 Raufa interviewed with the Middle East Youth Initiative about the progress in Yemen over the past 20 years. She explained that although women had more rights than previously, there was still much to improve on: "Women are working, but in rural areas which represent 70 percent of the population they work in family farms and are not being paid."[30]

information and mass communication. When Raufa returned from her freshman year, she no longer wore a veil. This came as a shock to her family and friends, who were even more amazed when she appeared on television without her veil. Soon Raufa became well-known throughout the country for her controversial unveiled television broadcasts.

Raufa continued her education and her work as a women's rights advocate. In 1977 she restarted the Yemeni Women's Association and became its president two years later. She eventually earned a master's degree in mass communication from Norwich University and a doctorate from the University of Paris.

Raufa worked as a professor and a leader in the campaign for women's rights. In 1993 she ran for Parliament in Yemen's first democratic elections. Though she lost, she continued to make a difference in Yemeni politics, inspiring women to be more politically active. She founded the Women's Studies Center at Sana'a University, and she helped form the Arab Democratic Institute, to promote women's voting projects and encourage Yemeni women, especially those in rural areas, to use their votes and let their voices be heard.

In 2011 Raufa died in a hospital in Cairo. Her death was mourned around the world by people who had been touched by her activism. Raufa made progress in her attempts to give Yemeni women more power, but the women of Yemen still have a tough road ahead of them. Traditionally, women's roles have been restrictive and submissive. Even today, girls in Yemen are often encouraged to marry in their teens, setting motherhood as their only lifetime goal and hoping for many children. Education, careers, and anything that takes girls or women into the public is often discouraged or even forbidden. Illiteracy among Yemeni women is still disturbingly high.

From an early age, Raufa showed independence and leadership in promoting women's rights, a cause to which she devoted much of her life. Her achievements made her one of the most important and influential feminists in the Arab world. She challenged the ways in which her choices were restricted, and she expanded what is possible for women in her country.

HOW WILL YOU ROCK THE WORLD?

I will rock the world by cleaning up and picking up trash outside of my house. I'll also turn off all the lights when I'm not using them. But the most important thing is I'll be helping others if they need help. We should do more things to help the world and help others.

SIERRA LOPEZ ☼ AGE 12

Rigoberta Menchú

1959– ❀ ACTIVIST ❀ GUATEMALA

*Rigoberta Menchú Tum appeals to the best in all of us,
wherever we live and whatever our background.*

—THE NOBEL PEACE PRIZE COMMITTEE

Rigoberta's back ached as she bent to pick up the beans that had fallen off the coffee bushes. Up ahead she could see her mother picking with her baby brother, Nicholás, strapped to her back. Rigoberta was worried. They had been at this *finca* (large coffee, cotton, or sugar cane plantation) for fifteen days now, and Nicholás had been crying the whole time. He was crying now. Her mother unwrapped him and tried to feed him some healing herbs. His belly was swollen from malnutrition, and he was barely breathing.

Eight-year-old Rigoberta could hardly contain her anger. Working on the fincas, they could hardly afford to buy food, let alone medicine for a sick baby. They couldn't ask for help because they spoke a

At Rigoberta's birth, a midwife tied red thread around her hands and feet, symbolizing her purity and to remind Rigoberta to care for the earth. Around Rigoberta's neck she tied a small red pouch containing herbs, plants, salt, lime, tobacco, and garlic to protect the girl from harm.

~~~

different language from the other workers. But most unfair was that if her mother stopped working to care for Nicholás, they would all be thrown out and would lose the money they desperately needed for food. When Nicholás died later that morning, Rigoberta was angrier than she'd ever been in her entire life. The day of his death was the first day of her battle to save her Indian people from their tremendous struggles.

Rigoberta Menchú was born in 1959, in the mountains of northwest Guatemala. She and her seven siblings grew up in the village of Chimel, which her parents founded. Like most of the people in Guatemala, Rigoberta's family and village were descended from the ancient and proud Mayan Indians of Central America. The families in her village were very poor, living in small huts built from cane or corn stalks. The villagers spent years clearing fields out of the forest just to grow enough corn to feed their families. But most years they couldn't live off their meager crops, so they were forced to work on the fincas that were owned by the Ladinos (people descended from the Spanish who had invaded Central America in the 1500s).

Although most Guatemalans are Indian, it was the Ladinos who controlled most of the country's land and businesses. Like most Indian children, Rigoberta never had a chance to go to school. As soon as she could walk, she helped her parents at the fincas. She picked up fallen coffee or cotton behind her mother, or watched her younger siblings so her mother could pick more. By eight, Rigoberta was

The first time Rigoberta went to the capital, she asked her father, "What are those strange animals on the road?" He answered, "Those are cars!"

~~~

working full time—meaning from three in the morning until the sun went down. For her fifteen-hour day she was paid about four cents!

Conditions were terrible. Although workers earned just enough to stay alive, the finca owners would cut their pay if they broke a branch off a coffee bush. They could buy extra food, medicine, and other necessities at the company store, but for much higher prices than normal. The result was that many workers earned no money at all after their months of hard labor, and many actually went into debt to pay for food. Workers who complained were fired. Rigoberta lost two brothers on the fincas; a younger one died of malnutrition, and an older one died from being sprayed with toxic pesticides (finca owners usually didn't clear workers from the fields before they sprayed).

When the families returned to their mountain villages to work their own fields, they faced even more difficult problems. They spent years clearing land and tending fields before they could finally produce enough to feed the families. That's just when the rich landowners stepped in, claiming the land was really theirs. The Indians would have to leave or work on the land as laborers.

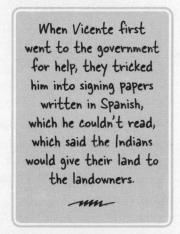

When Vicente first went to the government for help, they tricked him into signing papers written in Spanish, which he couldn't read, which said the Indians would give their land to the landowners.

As the village leader, Rigoberta's father, Vicente, protested. Rigoberta often traveled with her father to the capital, Guatemala City, as he met with members of the government and asked for help. They didn't care about the problems of the Indians, so Vicente met with labor organizations that really were trying to help the workers. Through them, Rigoberta came to believe that the only way the Indians could protect themselves from the government and the rich landowners would be to organize and fight for their rights. Rigoberta's father encouraged her. He often told her, "When you're old enough, you...must do what I do."

Her father was first arrested for his role in organizing the Indians when Rigoberta was just thirteen. Over the next few years, life became a nightmare. The government and landowners sent armies into villages. They destroyed everything, killing men, women, and children. They imprisoned and tortured anyone who fought back. They even forced young Indian men to fight against their own people, or be killed.

By the time she was fifteen, Rigoberta had taken over as a leader of her people. She met with her father's friends and with priests and Europeans. She organized her own village to protect itself from army raids. Of course, there was no money for defense, but they were creative. They developed underground escape routes, secret hideouts, and booby traps. The villagers learned to defend themselves with sticks, rocks, and other crude weapons.

> Villagers used lime juice, salt, and chilies to blind their attackers.

Once her own village was prepared, Rigoberta began traveling to other villages to teach them to fight back. As she traveled, Rigoberta began to realize that the biggest obstacle keeping Indians from organizing was their language. The Mayan Indians spoke twenty-two different languages, and few people spoke Spanish, so communicating with each other and protesting Spanish laws were nearly impossible. Over the next few years, Rigoberta learned to speak three other main Mayan languages, and she improved her Spanish with help from the Catholic nuns in the villages. She now had the tools she needed to be the voice of her people.

By 1978, when she was nineteen, Rigoberta and her entire family were being hunted by the government. They were all involved in fighting for Indian rights. Earlier her father had helped start the Committee of Peasant Unity, or CUC, which fought for fair wages and decent treatment from the landowners, and demanded respect for Indian communities, religion, and culture. When Rigoberta joined the CUC in 1979, it had grown into a powerful political group supported by the majority of Guatemalans.

It was too dangerous for the entire family to stay together, so the village had a special fiesta in honor of the Menchú family and to say good-bye. They ate a feast of roast pig and tamales, played drums and marimbas, and danced late into the night. It was one of the happiest memories of Rigoberta's difficult life. The next morning, they all scattered to different villages. It was the last time Rigoberta would see her family together and alive.

First her younger brother, Petrocinio, was tortured and burned to death while Rigoberta and her mother watched helplessly. Four months later, her father was killed during a protest in the capital. He and other CUC members took over several radio stations, trying to broadcast their story to the outside world. When they took over the Spanish embassy, still trying to get the world's attention, the army bombed the building. Everyone inside died. And finally, the next year, Rigoberta's mother was kidnapped and killed while out buying food for hungry villagers.

The Indian people of Guatemala now looked to Rigoberta to guide them. She became a leader of the CUC, organizing more protests in the capital and self-defense workshops in the villages. Everywhere Rigoberta went, she was hunted. The kidnappings and killings continued: by 1980 one hundred thousand Indians had been killed, thirty thousand were missing, and another two hundred thousand had fled to Mexico. In 1981, at twenty-two, Rigoberta, fearing for her life, joined her people in exile. She fled to Mexico. It broke her heart to leave her struggling people behind, but it was the only way she could spread their story to the outside world. If she did, she knew she could get the help the Indians needed to survive.

In Mexico she led the efforts to stop the Guatemalans' brutal treatment of the Indians. She began traveling the world telling of her people's struggle. Finally in 1983 the whole world heard the voice of the Guatemalan Indians, through the publication of *I, Rigoberta Menchú*, a book about Rigoberta's life. It was a huge hit and was published in twelve languages. In 1992 the little girl who'd picked coffee beans off the ground won the Nobel Peace Prize for her efforts on behalf of her people. She was the youngest person ever to win the world's most prestigious prize.

Thanks to Rigoberta's leadership and the courage of her people, conditions in Guatemala have improved. She

> Eighty-seven percent of Guatemalans still live in poverty.

used the $1.2 million Nobel award to start the Rigoberta Menchú Tum Foundation. Its mission is to continue helping native peoples improve their communities. With the world's outraged attention focused on Guatemala, the government was forced to stop most of its attacks and kidnappings. Recent governments have worked with Rigoberta and Indian groups to address their concerns.

With Guatemala's problems improving, Rigoberta finally felt she could spare enough of herself to fall in love and get married, something she thought she would never do. But Rigoberta has not rested. Instead she has turned her attention to the indigenous (native) peoples all over the world. "We have broken the silence around Guatemala. Now I would like to see native and non-native people living side by side," she said. In 1993 Rigoberta was chosen by the United Nations to be a Goodwill Ambassador for the Indigenous Peoples. In 2009 Rigoberta and her foundation began working to establish a Mayan University for Guatemalan Indians.

Rigoberta's work is far from finished. As long as there is injustice, Rigoberta will continue to be the brave voice for the oppressed, impoverished peoples of the world.

ROCK ON!

FRANCIA SIMON

Francia Simon was almost denied the right to an education. In the Dominican Republic, where she lives, all children are required to present birth certificates before they can enroll in school. But not everyone in the country has a birth certificate, especially not refugees. Francia worked hard to get her own documentation so she could go to school, and now she works with other children to help them do the same. In 2010 Francia's activism was rewarded with the International Children's Peace Prize, which was presented to her by Rigoberta Menchú.

Maya Lin

1959– ◈ ARCHITECT ◈ UNITED STATES

*You cannot ever forget that war
is not just a victory or loss.
It's really about individual lives.*

—MAYA LIN, DISCUSSING HER DESIGN FOR THE VIETNAM MEMORIAL

Professor Burr talked on and on. Maya loved her architecture class and thought Burr was brilliant, but some days her mind wandered—especially on beautiful spring days like this one. The students rustled in their chairs when a stranger entered the lecture hall and handed a message to the professor. As he read it, his face changed: a look of shock swept across his features. He cleared his throat and made an announcement.

"The Vietnam War veterans have chosen their winner for the memorial competition . . ."

Maya and the other students wondered why they brought this message to class. They had each entered a design into the contest for a new national monument in Washington, D.C., to honor Vietnam veterans, but it was just a class assignment—everyone knew a professional architect would win, not a student. Why not let them read about the winner in the newspaper, like everyone else?

" . . . and the winner is our own Maya Lin!"

The entire room gasped, including Maya. How could it be? Maya was just a college senior, with no real architecture experience. Her design was strange, unlike any memorials the students had ever seen. In fact, Professor Burr had given her a B for her work. And yet she had won over almost 1,500 entries. Professor Burr walked up to Maya and shook her hand.

"Congratulations, Maya," he said cheerfully, trying to hide his disappointment. He, too, had entered the contest. This young, inexperienced student had beaten him.

This was the first day of Maya's professional architecture career. She would go on to design some of the most original and beloved monuments in America. But her passion for designing and building began when she was a much younger girl.

Maya's parents fled China in the late 1940s. Her mother left with just one hundred-dollar bill pinned to the lining of her jacket. When they arrived in America, both were hired by Ohio University; her father became an art professor, and her mother worked as a professor of Oriental and English literature. Once settled in Athens, Ohio, they had a son and then a daughter, Maya.

Maya and her brother grew up on the college campus in a stimulating, artistic environment. "My parents very much brought us up to decide what we wanted to do," Maya said. "Maybe that is an Eastern philosophy—that you don't force an opinion on a child." Later in life, Maya explored many career directions, but even as a young girl, she was fascinated by architecture. She spent many hours in her room building miniature towns out of paper and scraps from her father's art studio.

When Maya graduated from high school, she was accepted at Yale University, where she studied architecture and sculpture. Her professors wanted her to choose one or the other, but Maya refused. She felt that learning about sculpture improved her architecture skills and vice versa. She said, "Architecture . . . is like writing a book. Everything in a building matters, from the doorknobs to the paint details. And sculpture is like writing a poem. You're not saying as much. It's an idea stripped bare."[31] Even now, Maya still uses sculpture to create her architectural designs. First, she builds tiny models, and then she makes detailed drawings from those models.

> Maya Lin's first name comes from a Hindu goddess, the mother of Buddha, and her last name means "forest."
>
> ~~~

During her junior year, Maya studied architecture in Europe. She noticed that Europeans went to the beautiful, park-like cemeteries not just to mourn, but also to enjoy the peaceful surroundings. They went there to relax and escape from the busy cities. "I've always been intrigued with death," she explained, "and man's relation to it." She realized that death was all around, and people had to seek ways to deal with their grief and find peace.

Back at Yale for her senior year, Maya put her insights to good use on an intriguing class assignment: to design a memorial honoring those who had died in the Vietnam War. The winning design would be built in the Constitution Gardens of Washington, DC. There were only two requirements for the design: (1) the names of the fifty-eight thousand soldiers killed or missing in action should be included, and (2) it should be in harmony with the landscape (it would go between the Lincoln Memorial and the Washington Monument). The selection committee also hoped the design would help America heal the pain of this controversial war.

Before starting on her entry, Maya walked around Constitution Gardens, studying every detail of the location. She asked herself questions like, "How can the relatives of people killed in Vietnam recover from their loss?" and "How can America recover from the war?" Her answer was to create a design that would encourage people to look at their pain, admit their losses, and always remember the war and those who died in it. The design Maya turned in was of two long, black granite walls joined at the center in a 130-degree angle—it looked a bit like two sides of a triangle. Every soldier's name would be carved into the walls, but the shiny black granite would reflect the image of the viewer. It was as if by looking at the names, visitors would be examining themselves. Since other D.C. monuments were generally realistic statues of people, Maya's design was unusual, to say the least.

When she first beat out the 1,420 other entries, people were excited that a young woman had won. But her design quickly became a flashpoint for America's still conflicted emotions about the war. Some people liked Maya's haunting sculpture, but others were upset that it didn't look the way they thought a patriotic war memorial should look. The *Chicago Tribune* said it was "bizarre" and the *New York Times* called it "a black gash of shame."

Powerful men in Washington began speaking out against Maya's entry. Secretary of the Interior James Watt, Texas billionaire Ross Perot, and Senator Jeremiah Denton all fought to stop the project. They were not excited about Maya's unique vision; in fact, one big complaint was that all the other Washington monuments were white but this one was black. They even criticized Maya, complaining that since she was a young woman who didn't fight in Vietnam, she couldn't possibly understand the meaning of the war.

In spite of the public conflict, Maya defended her design and refused to change it. She knew the public would respond to it if it were built. Jan Scruggs, the veteran who led the drive to create the memorial, said of Maya's courage, "She really believed in this design.... The strength of her own convictions carried us through quite a few conflicts." Against Maya's wishes, a compromise was reached: a second memorial would be built near Maya's site. It was a traditional statue of three soldiers, designed by Frederick Hart. Hart was paid $200,000 for his design; Maya was paid $20,000.

Maya wanted only the names of Vietnam soldiers on the wall. She even refused to put her own name on it. It's behind the wall, out of public view.

When her wall was finally built in 1982, it became an overnight sensation. The critics were silenced. Finally, the nation had a focus for the past thirty years of unresolved grief and anger over Vietnam. The reflective sculpture encouraged visitors to deal with their repressed emotions about Vietnam, and it helped everyone grieve. Visitors leave flowers and mementos below the names of loved ones and even make pencil impressions of the names onto paper to take home with them. The award committee praised its impact: "This one superb design has changed the way war memorials—and monuments as a whole—are perceived." Maya was honored with the 1988 Presidential Design Award, but more important to her, the Vietnam Memorial is now the most visited memorial in the United States.

> Visitors are often surprised at how warm the Wall is to the touch—as if it were alive (the black granite holds the warmth of the sun).
> ⸺

After the Wall, Maya vowed never to do another memorial because of the controversy she'd endured over the Vietnam Memorial. But when she was asked to design the Civil Rights Memorial, she couldn't refuse. The monument honors the people who fought for equality during the Civil Rights movement of the 1950s and 1960s— from well-known leaders like Rosa Parks and Martin Luther King Jr. to forgotten heroes. Maya studied history books and the speeches of Dr. King to come up with another innovative design: a black granite wall carved with a quote from Dr. King and veiled by a thin sheet of water flowing over it into a pool. In front of the wall is a large black granite disk inscribed with a chronology of events from the Civil Rights era, from the outlawing of school segregation to the assassination of Dr. King.

Maya continues to work as an architect and has added many new memorials and public sculptures to her portfolio. Her designs never overpower the audience or the space. Their goal is not to intimidate or to lecture, but to inspire people to stop and think. She wants her work to stir emotions in people. The Vietnam Memorial has not only stirred the emotions of hundreds of thousands of visitors, it has also helped Americans come to terms with their conflicting emotions about the war and heal its wounds. She has since designed several more memorials and buildings, including the *What Is Missing?* installation and the Museum of Chinese in America. She has received awards from the National Endowment for the Arts, the American Academy in Rome, the American Academy of Arts and Letters, and more. Maya has already left her mark on the world—a mark of peace and reconciliation.

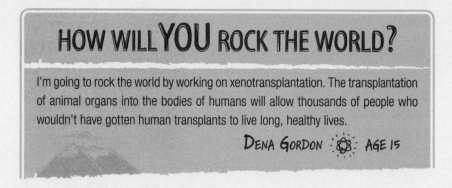

HOW WILL YOU ROCK THE WORLD?

I'm going to rock the world by working on xenotransplantation. The transplantation of animal organs into the bodies of humans will allow thousands of people who wouldn't have gotten human transplants to live long, healthy lives.

DENA GORDON ·⊛· AGE 15

MidoRi Goto

1971– ☼ VIOLINIST ☼ JAPAN AND UNITED STATES

*As musicians we're trained to be self critical so we can
get better. But fundamentally we love music. It's a love
that drives us to practice and keep working at it.
It's something I love so much and gives me so much joy.*

—MIDORI GOTO

Fourteen-year-old Midori stood at the front of the stage near
famous composer and conductor Leonard Bernstein. Surrounded
by the musicians of the Boston Symphony Orchestra, she was
the featured violin soloist for a concert at the Tanglewood Music
Festival. The festival was held outdoors, and the summer night was
hot and humid. Despite the less-than-ideal playing conditions, Midori
had already been sensational through four movements of Bernstein's
difficult *Serenade for Violin, String Orchestra, Harp, and Percussion.*
As the fifth and final movement began, Midori continued to impress
the audience with playing that the *New York Times* would later call

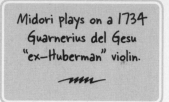

Midori plays on a 1734 Guarnerius del Gesu "ex–Huberman" violin.

"technically near-perfect," an amazing feat given the challenge of the piece.

Then, partway through the last movement, Midori faced an incident that every violinist dreads: a string broke on her violin. Handling the situation with her typical calmness, she turned to the concertmaster (the person who leads the violin section and serves as assistant to the conductor) and borrowed his violin. Though the concertmaster's violin was noticeably larger than Midori's and very different from the instrument she was used to, she played on in the *Serenade* with only a very brief pause.

Crisis seemed to be averted, and the orchestra continued its performance. Just moments later, though, the unthinkable happened: another string broke! Again Midori exchanged violins, this time getting yet another unfamiliar instrument that was larger than her own. Unfazed by these setbacks that could fluster even the most experienced musician, Midori continued to play seamlessly through the final note. When the music ended, the audience and Midori's fellow performers erupted into a loud, cheering ovation for the young violinist. They may not have known it at the time, but they had just seen one of the most famous performances ever given by this musician who would go on to become a worldwide sensation.

Midori Goto—who is known professionally by the one-word name Midori—was born in Osaka, Japan, on October 25, 1971. Even as a toddler, Midori knew that she wanted to play the violin, and her first instrument was a gift that she asked for on her third birthday. By the age of four, Midori was studying music with her mother, who was also a violinist.

In the early 1980s, Midori and her mother moved to the United States, and Midori began training with renowned teacher Dorothy DeLay at the world-famous Juilliard School of Music. When Midori was just eleven, she made her concert debut at the New York Philharmonic's New Year's Eve Gala. She wasn't originally on the program, but the orchestra's music director was so impressed with her talent that he included her as a guest soloist at the last minute. Her legendary performance at

226

Tanglewood happened just a few years later. Midori has since performed thousands of concerts all around the world, sometimes up to one hundred in a year! She also started recording music at the age of fourteen, and she now has more than a dozen albums to her credit.

Midori's book, SIMPLY MIDORI, was published in German in 2004.

When she was fifteen, Midori left Juilliard and started to study the violin on her own. Her independent explorations into music helped her develop a unique approach and perspective as a violinist. About this time in her life, Midori said, "It all started to come together: the knowledge of history and culture and theory, the experience of playing in concerts, as well as personal experiences. . . . It made me really think for myself; that's what was so good about it. I had to be my own teacher, to develop my ears, to be very critical."[32]

Midori continued to grow as a musician throughout her career, and her success carries on today. In addition to performing, she now teaches and is currently the Jascha Heifetz Chair in Violin at the University of Southern California's Thornton School of Music. She also spends much of her time working with community organizations. "I was always interested in education," Midori said. "Not just receiving, but also helping others and being part of the community."[33] In 1992 she founded Midori & Friends, with the goal of encouraging children to engage with music. Based in New York City, this nonprofit foundation works with public schools and gives students the opportunity to explore music through concerts, workshops, and other activities. In her native Japan, Midori started a similar organization called Music Sharing. She has also founded groups that support youth orchestras and help bring world-class music to small communities. In 2007 Midori's community engagement activities were recognized on a global level when she was named a United Nations Messenger of Peace. As a peace messenger, Midori has helped bring attention to the UN's work toward improving people's lives around the world.

You might think that a young person with as much talent as Midori would have focused almost solely on music-related activities, but Midori has always nurtured other interests too. As a teen, she was fascinated by history and archeology. She has always liked to read, and she also enjoys writing and theater. In college, Midori majored in psychology and gender studies, and she earned both a bachelor's and a master's degree.

As a young girl, Midori's wide-ranging interests not only gave her a well-rounded background to bring to her music, but they also ensured that she didn't feel stuck with going into one specific field. A couple of days after her performance on that summer night at Tanglewood, after proving herself to be one of the most talented young musicians in the world, fourteen-year-old Midori spoke to a reporter about her plans. "I'm not sure yet what I want to do," she said. "I think I'll be a writer, or an archaeologist—or maybe a violinist."[34] While any one of those options would likely have led to a rewarding career, thousands of music lovers around the world are lucky that she chose the last.

HOW WILL YOU ROCK THE WORLD?

I will rock the world by playing in an orchestra or band. I already play the clarinet in several bands and have played the piano at the New York Botanical Gardens and at Carnegie Hall three times.!

TERLENDA CRAWFORD · AGE 12

Natalie Portman

1981– ⚬ ACTRESS ⚬ ISRAEL AND UNITED STATES

*It's always fun to do something different;
challenge yourself in new ways.*

—NATALIE PORTMAN

Natalie stepped outside into the snow and rested her mittened hands on the picket fence. In jeans and a warm plaid coat, with her brown hair pulled back from her face, Natalie looked like any other teenager on a winter morning. If she weren't surrounded by a camera crew, someone might have said she looked like the average girl next door.

In fact, in this case, Natalie was the girl next door: she was acting in the role of Marty, the teenage neighbor of a character played by famous actor Timothy Hutton in the movie *Beautiful Girls*. As Natalie started delivering her lines—bantering with Hutton about his snow-shoveling abilities—her presence was confident and poised, despite the fact that she was only in her early teens.

The scene lasted just two and a half minutes, but in that short time Natalie managed to successfully establish the off-beat character that she'd play for the rest of the movie. When the film premiered, her performance earned rave reviews and even nominations for Best Supporting Actress and Most Promising Actress from the Chicago Film Critics Association! Though it wasn't Natalie's first movie role, it helped launch her career as one of today's most successful movie stars.

The actress the world knows as Natalie Portman was born Natalie Hershlag on June 9, 1981, in Jerusalem, Israel. (She would later adopt the stage name Portman to protect her family's privacy when she started acting.) Natalie's father is a fertility doctor, and her mother an artist. When Natalie was three, she and her parents moved to the United States, where they lived in Washington, DC, Connecticut, and then New York.

Natalie showed artistic talent from an early age, starting to study dance soon after she moved to the United States. She also attended theater camps and liked putting on performances with her neighborhood friends. Even as a child, Natalie had a riveting presence, and when she was eleven, an agent approached her in a pizza parlor and asked her to model for Revlon. She turned down the offer, though, in order to concentrate on acting. Her focus paid off when she got the opportunity to star in her first movie, *Léon: The Professional*, when she was only twelve years old. Natalie's debut movie tells the story of a girl who becomes apprenticed to a professional assassin after her parents are killed. While Natalie's performance in *Léon: The Professional* earned mostly positive reviews, some critics felt uneasy about the role because it brought up mature and violent themes, especially given the actor's young age.

Soon after her movie debut, Natalie landed parts in other films. Her role as precocious neighbor Marty in *Beautiful Girls* came in 1996, and critics were

Natalie is also a scientist! She has co-written two research papers that were published in scientific journals. She was also named a semifinalist in the prestigious Intel Science Talent Search.

again impressed with Natalie's performance—a *New York Times* review called her "scene-stealingly good" and "a budding knockout." By the late 1990s, Natalie was firmly established as a rising talent in the film world. Among other roles, she starred as a daughter who moves across the country with her mom in *Anywhere but Here* and as Queen Padmé Amidala in the Star Wars Prequel Trilogy. In the 2000s, Natalie starred in such movies as *Garden State, Closer, V for Vendetta,*

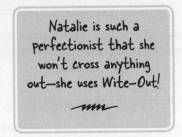

Natalie is such a perfectionist that she won't cross anything out—she uses Wite-Out!

Mr. Magorium's Wonder Emporium, The Other Boleyn Girl, Brothers, and *Black Swan,* among others. It should be noted that Natalie has played a variety of film roles, and many of these movies are best suited for mature audiences.

Natalie has never shied away from challenging parts, and her success in a wide range of roles speaks to her versatility as an actress. She works hard to prepare for every movie. For her part in *V for Vendetta,* Natalie shaved her head and studied with a voice coach to perfect a British accent, practicing by speaking with the accent all the time in her day-to-day life. For *Black Swan* she trained in ballet for up to eight hours a day and continued with her role despite a rib injury and a concussion. Natalie immerses herself in her roles and says, "It's one of the best things about acting—living someone else's life and their experiences, to see what the world is like through their eyes."[35]

Natalie's work has earned well-deserved acclaim, including an Academy Award, Golden Globe Awards, a Screen Actors Guild Award, a BAFTA (British Academy of Film and Television Arts) Award, and many other honors. Natalie's accomplishments extend beyond the screen to the stage, too; she starred as the title character in the play *The Diary of Anne Frank* and played a role in *The Seagull* by Anton Chekov. She has also started to work as a producer, founding a production company called HandsomeCharlie Films.

Throughout her life, Natalie has devoted herself to education, and she has excelled in her studies just as she's thrived as an actor. She took advanced placement curriculum at her public high school on Long

Island, New York, and she even missed the New York premiere of *Star Wars: Episode I—The Phantom Menace* to study for high school finals! Natalie went on to Harvard University, where she earned a degree in psychology and restricted her movie work to summer breaks in order to concentrate on her studies. Since graduating from Harvard, Natalie has taken classes at the Hebrew University of Jerusalem. She speaks Hebrew and English and has also studied Arabic, French, German, and Japanese.

Natalie is passionate about many social issues. She believes strongly in animal rights and has been a vegetarian since age eight. She avoids wearing or using animal products like fur, leather, and feathers and has even started her own shoe line featuring footwear that does not use any products from animals.

Another important cause for Natalie is helping impoverished people around the world earn enough money to take care of themselves and their families. Natalie has worked with international organizations that provide banking programs for families in developing countries. As part of their work, these groups offer small loans called microloans to help people—most often women—start their own businesses and earn a living.

Natalie has generally preferred to keep her personal life private, but it's clear that she's close to her parents and that family has always been important to her. At the age of thirty, Natalie started a family of her own with fiancé Benjamin Millepied, a ballet dancer she met on the set of *Black Swan*. The couple welcomed a baby boy in the summer of 2011.

While Natalie has now added the role of mom to her life, we can look forward to continuing to see her on the screen as well. Her work is always evolving, and with her intelligence, creativity, and love for learning, she will always be setting new challenges for herself and meeting them with success.

ROCK ON!

ABIGAIL BRESLIN

Abigail Breslin started her acting career when she was only three years old! She acted in several commercials, and then when she was five, she got a role in her first movie, *Signs*. When she played Olive in *Little Miss Sunshine*, she was nominated for an Academy Award for Best Supporting Actress, making her one of the youngest Oscar nominees in history. Abigail is known for her ability to bring her characters to life, and she'll surely continue rocking the world on the big screen.

Ashley Rhodes-Courter

1985– ✦ AUTHOR AND ADVOCATE ✦ UNITED STATES

I applaud Ashley for bravely sharing her
story and commend this young woman for
her on-going efforts to help the children
in the foster care system.

—SUZANNE BUCKINGHAM SLADE, AUTHOR

Seventeen-year-old Ashley was on a mission. She was determined to go to college, but she had hardly any money to do it. She'd been adopted a few years ago, and her adoptive parents, Phil and Gay Courter, gave her so much, including a safe, loving home, but they didn't have the money to pay for her college. So she decided she would win money by entering writing contests.

The moment she read the call for submissions to the *New York Times Magazine* writing contest, prompting her to describe her most powerful day, Ashley knew exactly which day she would write about: her adoption day.

Recently she had settled in to the deep cushions of the sectional couch next to her adoptive parents. Bright light streamed in from the tall windows overlooking the Crystal River in Florida, but she was focused on the television screen across the room. She felt a flurry of butterflies in her stomach as the court video started to play and she saw herself come onscreen. When the judge on the video turned to twelve-year-old Ashley and asked, "Do you want to be adopted?" the Ashley on-screen shrugged and said, "I guess so."

It was no Little Orphan Annie response, but that's what made it all the more powerful. Adoption is complicated, especially for a twelve-year-old girl who has lived in fourteen foster homes in the last nine years, has dealt with forty-four caseworkers, twenty-three attorneys, nineteen foster parents, three abuse registry workers, and four judges. She was finally being invited into a permanent home, but how could she know this was really the best thing for her? To Ashley Rhodes, life was too full of turmoil to be excited about moving into yet another home.

When Ashley had written her contest submission, she titled it "Three Little Words," for the three words she said to the judge that day, and sent it off, full of hope that she could win some money to add to her college fund. When she learned that she had won the grand prize, she was elated! Her story appeared in the magazine, the check arrived in the mail, and before long, book publishers were calling Ashley to ask if she had written a book. Everyone wanted to hear her story.

> One of Ashley's foster parents made her run laps in the hot sun until she collapsed! This woman was later charged with abusing many of her foster children.

Her story was long and painful. When Ashley was three years old, her birth mother, stepfather, and little brother were moving to Florida. "We're moving to the Sunshine State to live happily ever after," Ashley's mother told her. But when they got to Florida, the police arrested her mother and stepfather and took Ashley and her brother to strange people's homes. Sometimes she lived in the same home as her brother, sometimes she didn't. For years, Ashley would wonder, *What have I done that was so terrible that I had to be taken from my mother?*

During her time in foster care, Ashley liked to write, but she never tried to write anything like a book. Mostly, she had written poems, songs, and journal entries—nothing that she ever intended to share with anyone else. Because she moved so much and often lived in homes with other foster children, who would steal or destroy her possessions, she didn't even have most of what she had written anymore. Still, she found comfort in the process of writing, and then she would memorize her poems and songs so she could always remember them. No one could steal them from her then.

One winter when Ashley was in fifth grade, her teacher asked Ashley to stay after class. Her teacher was kind but firm. If Ashley ever acted out for attention, the teacher did not allow it. But she also seemed to notice that Ashley was special. This day, she was not holding Ashley after class to reprimand her but to reward her. She opened her desk drawer and pulled out a book.

"It's *Anne of Green Gables*," she said, smiling.

It was the first book that Ashley ever owned. When she opened the cover, she noticed that the teacher had written on the title page, which made this gift even more special. Then when she read the book and discovered that the main character—a red-headed orphan whose name started with an A—had many similarities to herself, she felt connected, not just to Anne but also to her teacher and to the idea that words matter.

Now that she was seventeen and had just won a writing contest, Ashley had no doubt that words mattered. But that just made the pressure to write a book that much scarier.

> Through Shape What's to Come, Ashley hosted interviews at the 2010 TEDWomen Conference. "One of the really cool things about Shape What's to Come is that it really highlights the idea that ... women ... [are] no longer taking a linear path to school, careers, family," she said in her interview with Girl Scouts CEO Jessica Lawrence. In short, both women agree that girls can choose the future that's best for them—whether it's traditional or not.

237

"Don't worry," Gay said. "I'll help you."

Gay was a novelist, so she knew all about the writing process and what it would take for Ashley to publish a book. She also knew that if Ashley was going to write about her life, they'd have to get the files from the state that included everywhere that Ashley had lived in foster care. Together Ashley and Gay went through the case files and contacted Ashley's former foster homes. They compiled interviews and visited places that Ashley hadn't been to in years.

Once Ashley had written a rough draft of the book, she had other people read it to tell her what they thought. One of Gay's most frequent comments—and other readers agreed—was that Ashley needed to include more emotion in her book. This became her biggest challenge. "As a child, I was very closed off and tried not to let my emotions of rejection, sorrow, pain, guilt, and fear get the best of me," Ashley said, so it was hard for her to include emotions she never really let herself feel. But she knew the feedback was true, that readers wanted to see her emotions in her writing to they could connect with her through more than just her descriptions of place and action, so she revised often.

> The purpose of foster care is to provide a safe place for children to stay until they can be placed in a permanent, loving home—either with their family or with an adoptive family. Not all foster homes are bad, but many are less than ideal.

Ashley was clear that she didn't want her book to be an orphan sob story like so many other books are, though. She wanted her book to call readers to action, to be aware of the state of the welfare systems in their areas and the challenges that foster children face because of it. She also wanted the book to be a thank-you to all of the people who work with at-risk youth and try to make a difference in their lives. Most of those people do not get thanked for their hard work even though they work long hours to help children find safe homes.

Three Little Words was published in 2008, when Ashley Rhodes-Courter was twenty-three. It has been a *New York Times* bestseller, and Ashley used her book tour as an opportunity to raise awareness of the foster care system. She even hosted a television show called *Explore Adoption*, which aired in Florida. The show won an Emmy. Ashley is also an ambassador for Levi's Shape What's to Come women's empowerment community, and in 2011 she became an international correspondent for MTV.

In 2009, 424,000 children in America lived in foster homes.

With the money Ashley earned from her writing, she went to Eckerd College and graduated in 2008 with majors in communications and theater. Now Ashley's in graduate school at the University of Southern California studying social work while she is also a foster mother and continues to speak about foster care to audiences around the country.

HOW WILL YOU ROCK THE WORLD?

I'm going to rock the world by writing and publishing a book to help teens get over the stress they go through due to family, friends, and school. I know for a fact that the reason most slacking kids don't do their work in school is because of problems with friends or family. Teens need assurance and guidance that they can't always get from their school counselor. I feel safe using advice from a book, and I know others do too. This is how I'm going to rock the world.

EMILY ANN BRAKE ⚙ AGE 13

Recommended Resources

We have listed below the resources used to research the amazing girls profiled in this book and have also included some additional materials that you can check out if you want to know more about these heroines.

BOOKS

Ambrose, Stephen E. *Undaunted Courage: Meriwether Lewis, Thomas Jefferson, and the Opening of the American West.* New York: Touchstone, 1996.

Ashby, Ruth, and Deborah Gore Ohm, eds. *Herstory: Women Who Changed the World.* New York: Viking, 1995.

Baldwin, Louis. *Women of Strength: Biographies of 106 Who Have Excelled in Traditionally Male Fields.* Jefferson, NC: McFarland, 1996.

Barker-Benfield, G. J., and Catherine Clinton. *Portraits of American Women: From Settlement to the Present.* New York: St. Martin's Press, 1991.

Beckner, Chrisanne. *100 African-Americans Who Shaped American History.* San Francisco: Bluewood Books, 1995.

Biracree, Tom. *Wilma Rudolph, Women of Achievement Series.* New York: Chelsea House, 1988.

Borland, Kathryn Kilby. *Phillis Wheatley, Young Revolutionary Poet.* Indianapolis: Patria Press, Inc., 2005.

Brill, Marlene Targ. *Journey for Peace: The Story of Rigoberta Menchu*. New York: Lodestar Books, 1996.

Cosson, M. J. *Harriet Tubman*. Edina, MN: Abdo Publishing Company, 2007.

Daly, Jay. *Presenting S. E. Hinton*. New York: Dell, 1989.

Dee, Catherine. *The Girls' Book of Wisdom: Empowering, Inspirational Quotes from Over 400 Fabulous Females*. New York: Little, Brown Books for Young Readers, 1999.

Emboden, William. *Sarah Bernhardt*. New York: Macmillan, 1975.

Felder, Deborah G. *The 100 Most Influential Women of All Time: A Ranking Past and Present*. New York: Citadel Press, 1996.

Ferris, Jeri. *What I Had Was Singing: The Story of Marian Anderson*. Minneapolis: Carolrhoda Books, 1994.

Frank, Anne. *The Diary of a Young Girl: The Definitive Edition*. Edited by Otto Frank and Mirjam Pressler. Translated by Susan Massotty. New York: Doubleday, 1995.

Frazier, Neta Lohnes. *Path to the Pacific: The Story of Sacagawea*. New York: Sterling Publishing, 2007.

Greenblatt, Miriam. *Hatshepsut and Ancient Egypt*. New York: Benchmark Books, 2000.

Gupte, Pranay. *Mother India: A Political Biography of Indira Gandhi*. New York: Charles Scribner's Sons, 1992.

Hopping, Lorraine Jean. *Space Rocks: The Story of Planetary Geologist Adriana Ocampo*. New York: Scholastic, 2005.

Keller, Helen. *The Story of My Life*. Edited by John Albert Macy. New York: Doubleday, 1954.

Krull, Kathleen. *Wilma Unlimited: How Wilma Rudolph Became the World's Fastest Woman*. New York: Harcourt Brace, 1996.

Lazzarini, Roberta, and John Lazzarini, eds. *Pavlova: Portrait of a Dancer*. New York: Viking, 1984.

Leakey, Mary. *Disclosing the Past*. Garden City, NY: Doubleday, 1984.

MacDonald, Anne L. *Feminine Ingenuity: How Women Inventors Changed America*. New York: Ballantine, 1994.

Malone, Mary. *Maya Lin: Architect and Artist*. Springfield, NJ: Enslow Publishers, 1995.

McAuley, Karen. *Golda Meir*. New York: Chelsea House, 1985.

McGrayne, Sharon Bertsch. *Nobel Prize Women in Science: Their Lives, Struggles and Momentous Discoveries*. New York: Birch Lane Press, 1993.

Menchú, Rigoberta. *I, Rigoberta Menchú*. Edited by Elisabeth Burgos-Debray. Translated by Ann Wright. London: Verso, 1983.

Myles, Bruce. *Night Witches: The Amazing Story of Russia's Women Pilots in World War II*. Chicago: Academy Chicago Publishers, 1997.

Oliver, Paul. *Bessie Smith*. London: Cassell, 1959.

Pasaschoff, Naomi. *A Student's Guide to the Brontë Sisters*. Berkeley Heights, NJ: Enslow Publishers, 2009.

Perón, Eva. *My Mission in Life*. New York: Vantage Press, 1953.

Pflaum, Rosalynd. *Grand Obsession: Madame Curie and Her World*. New York: Doubleday, 1989.

Rolka, Gail Meyer. *100 Women Who Shaped World History*. San Francisco: Bluewood Rooks, 1994.

Sebba, Anne. *Mother Teresa: Beyond the Image*. New York: Doubleday, 1997.

Sellars, Jane. *Charlotte Brontë*. New York: Oxford University Press, 1997.

Shiels, Barbara. *Winners: Women and the Nobel Prize*. Minneapolis: Dillon, 1985.

Smith, Linda Irwin. *Women Who Write*. Los Angeles: Figueroa Press, 2008.

Stille, Darlene R. *Extraordinary Women of Medicine*. New York: Children's Press, 1997.

Stille, Darlene R. *Extraordinary Women Scientists*. Chicago: Children's Press, 1995.

Taylor, M. W. *Harriet Tubman*. New York: Chelsea House, 1991.

Vare, Ethlie Ann, and Greg Ptacek. *Women Inventors and Their Discoveries*. Minneapolis: Oliver Press, 1993.

Vigée-Le Brun, Elisabeth. *Memoirs of Madame Vigée-Lebrun*. Gloucester: Dodo Press, 2010.

Wallach, Janet. *Chanel: Her Style and Her Life*. New York: Nan A. Talese/ Doubleday, 1998.

Wepman, Denis. *Helen Keller, American Women of Achievement Series*. New York: Chelsea House, 1987.

Young, Bette Roth. *Emma Lazarus in Her World: Life and Letters*. Philadelphia: The Jewish Publication Society, 1995.

Zaharias, Babe Didrikson. *This Life I've Led: My Autobiography*. New York: A. S. Barnes, 1955.

WEBSITES

Girls Can Do Anything Magazine.
http://gcdamagazine.com/em/inspirational-girls.

Girl's World, A. "Women's History Treasure Hunt."
www.agirlsworld.com/amy/pajama/wmhistory/links.html.

Teen Ink.
teenink.com/.

Teen News Net.
www.teennewsnet.com/Amazing_Teens.html.

MOVIES

Coco Before Chanel, 2009, Anne Fontaine

The Diary of Anne Frank, 1959, George Stevens

Evita, 1996, Alan Parker

Florence Nightingale, 1985, Daryl Duke

Great Souls: Mother Teresa, 2002, Tom Ivy

Jane Eyre, 2011, Cary Fukanaga

Joan of Arc, 1999, Christian Duguay

The Journey of Sacagawea, 2004, PBS

The Life and Times of Frida Kahlo, 2005, Amy Stechler

Maya Lin: A Strong Clear Vision, 1994, Freida Lee Mock

Midori: Live at Carnegie Hall, 2006, Midori

The Miracle Worker, 2000, Nadia Tass

The Outsiders, 1983, Francis Ford Coppola

Temple Grandin, 2010, Mick Jackson

Tex, 1982, Tim Hunter

A Woman Called Moses, 1978, Paul Wendkos

Wuthering Heights, 1992, Peter Kosminsky

A Woman Called Golda, 1982, Alan Gibson

Endnotes

1. The ages of the individuals who gave quotes for the "How Will You Rock" sections of this book reflect the age of the person at the time the quote was given.

2. Tuyet A. Tran and Chu V. Nguyen, Accessed May 10, 2011. "Trung Trac & Trung Nhi," Viettouch.com: http://www.viettouch.com/trungsis/.

3. The information presented in all Rock On spotlights was gathered from public sources.

4. Sor Juana Ines de la Cruz, *A Sor Juana Anthology*, trans. Alan S. Trueblood (Cambridge, MA: Harvard University Press, 1988), 178.

5. Elisabeth Vigée-Le Brun, *The Memoirs of Elisabeth Vigée-Le Brun*, trans. Siân Evans (Indianapolis: Indiana University Press, 1989), 11.

6. Vigée-Le Brun, 32.

7. Vigée-Le Brun, 2.

8. M. W. Taylor, *Harriet Tubman: Antislavery Activist* (New York and Philadelphia: Chelsea House, 1991), 37.

9. Anne Macdonald, *Feminine Ingenuity: Women and Invention in America* (New York: Ballantine, 1992), 51.

10. Giraud Chester, *Embattled Maiden: The Life of Anna Dickinson* (New York: G. P. Putnam's Sons, 1951), 93–94.

11. Emma Lazarus, *Poems of Emma Lazarus* (Boston: Houghton Mifflin, 1899), 202–3.

12. Helen Keller, *The Story of My Life*, ed. John Albert Macy (New York: Doubleday, 1954), 21–22.

13. James Farmer, *Eleanor Roosevelt* (PBS, Portland, OR: 1999).

14. A. H. Wood and Elizabeth Wood Ellem, "Queen Salote Tupou III," in *Friendly Islands: A History of Tonga*, ed. Noel Rutherford (Melbourne, Australia: Oxford University Press, 1977), 209.

15. Andre Breton, "Frida Kahlo de Rivera," in *Frida Kahlo and Tina Modotti*, ed. Mark Francis (London: Whitechapel Art Gallery, 1982), 36.

16. Breton, 37.

17. Marguerite Holloway, "Mary Leakey: Unearthing History," *Scientific American* (October 1994): http://www.scientificamerican.com/article.cfm?id=mary-leakey-unearthing-hi&page=2.

18. Mary Leakey, *Disclosing the Past* (Garden City, NY: Doubleday, 1984), 193.

19. Babe Didrikson Zaharias, *This Life I've Led: My Autobiography* (New York: A. S. Barnes, 1955), 88–89.

20. Zaharias, 27, 76.

21. Indira Gandhi, *Letters to an American Friend: 1950–1984*, ed. Dorothy Norman (San Diego: Harcourt Brace Jovanovich, 1985), 178–79.

22. Anne Frank, *The Diary of a Young Girl: The Definitive Edition*, ed. Otto Frank and Mirjam Pressler, trans. Susan Massotty (New York: Doubleday, 1995), 1.

23. Frank, 281.

24. Tom Biracree, *Wilma Rudolph, Women of Achievement Series* (New York: Chelsea House, 1988), 107.

25. Bruce Myles, *Night Witches: The Untold Story of Soviet Women in Combat* (Novato, California: Presidio, 1981), 6.

26. Harold Stockton, Dariusz Tyminski, and Christer Bergström, "Marina Raskova and Soviet Female Pilots," WWII Ace Stories (9 December 1998): http://www.elknet.pl/acestory/raskov/raskov.htm.

27. Stockton.

28. Myles, 145.

29. The World Bank Group, "Gender Stats, Middle East and North Africa," 2011, http://stats.uis.unesco.org/unesco/TableViewer/document.aspx?ReportId=124&IF_Language=eng&BR_Country=8850&BR_Region=40525

30. Diana Greenwald, "Gender, Development and Governance in Yemen, 20 Years On," *Middle East Youth Initiative* (17 June 2010): http://www.shababinclusion.org/content/blog/detail/1615/.

31. Bob Italia, *Maya Lin: Honoring Our Forgotten Heroes* (Minneapolis: Abdo & Daughters, 1993), 7–9.

32. Hal Leonard Corporation, *21st Century Violinists* (San Rafael, CA: String Letter Publishing, 1999), 55.

33. CNN Entertainment, "Midori Goto: From Prodigy to Peace Ambassador" (3 November 2008): http://articles.cnn.com/ 2008-11 -03/entertainment/ta.midori_1_prodigy-musical-education-juilliard -school?_s=PM:SHOWBIZ.

34. Tim Page, "Unpretentious Prodigy Puzzled by All the Fuss," *New York Times* (29 July 1986): sec. c, p. 11.

35. Joe Neumaier, "Natalie Portman Is Finally Shedding Her 'Wise Old Teen' Image," *Daily News* (25 July 2004): http://articles.nydailynews .com/2004-07-25/entertainment/18273438_1_child-actor-stage-door -manor-characters/3.